Praise for *Last Nerve*

"Mindy Uhrlaub's powerful and inspiring memoir is a work of courageous transformation. She deepens her soul by turning her pain into power and ardently committing herself to the struggle against ALS for the legacy of her mother, for herself, and for all those suffering from the disease. We are grateful."

—V (FORMERLY EVE ENSLER), author of
The Vagina Monologues and *Reckoning*

"A profound story about a family finding strength in themselves and in one another while courageously facing all that life could throw at them. *Last Nerve* makes a powerful statement about confronting our personal monsters and how growth and transcendence are forged in the act of confronting."

—FERNANDO VIEIRA, MD, CEO and
chief scientific officer of the ALS
Therapy Development Institute

"For anyone who ever thought she faced an insurmountable life challenge, anyone who ever asked herself, "Why me?" or pulled the covers over her head when hard luck hit her, here comes an essential book. Faced with what many would see as a crushing diagnosis, Mindy Uhrlaub has delivered a story overflowing with optimism, positive energy, humor, and downright joy. I will carry her story with me forever."

—JOYCE MAYNARD, author of
At Home in the World and *The Best of Us*

"*Last Nerve* is a singularly courageous exploration of what it means to face adversity head-on. Writing with breathtaking honesty, Mindy Uhrlaub takes us on a deeply compelling journey through resilience, love, and the unbreakable bonds of family, proving that all the best stories, like this one, are about hope."

—JANIS COOKE NEWMAN, author of
A Master Plan for Rescue and *Mary: Mrs. A. Lincoln*

"[Mindy's] book is an outstanding account of one brave family's experience with familial ALS, a severely incapacitating and life-limiting genetic neurologic condition. Their rising to the never-ending challenges of living with ALS, while fostering hope that meaningful treatments will be developed, is a source of inspiration to anyone dedicated to finding a cure for this devastating disease."

—JEROME KURENT, MD, MPH, professor of neurology
and medicine at the Medical University of South Carolina
and director of the Ralph H. Johnson Veterans Affairs
Medical Center's ALS Multidisciplinary Clinic

"The author's bulldog spirit summarizes it all. This beautifully written memoir shines light on her unrelenting courage and resilience to fight for societal and personal causes that are dear to her. It serves as a reminder for medical professionals to treat every individual with compassion and respect, because behind every individual seen in research or clinic lies a complex tapestry of arduous battles fought daily, unwavering love, and importantly, hope."

—SUMA BABU, MBBS, MPH, ALS neurologist
at Massachusetts General Hospital

"*Last Nerve* is a deeply moving, powerfully intimate, and courageous memoir that pulls readers through the trials of familial love, loss, and the emotional complexities of navigating life under the specter of ALS. Mindy's unflinching honesty as a mother, a wife, and a daughter facing devastating medical realities is both heart-wrenching and inspiring. With clear-eyed reflections on grief, resilience, and the hope for future cures, this memoir offers a poignant journey of personal and generational struggle, beautifully capturing the power of family and self-discovery. *Last Nerve* is a must-read for anyone facing the shadow of illness or loss and seeking to find strength in the face of it. It is a story of courage and healing that will linger in your heart long after you turn the final page."

—PAUL SAMPOGNARO, MD, neurologist
and assistant professor at the University
of California San Francisco

LAST
NERVE

A MEMOIR *of* ILLNESS *and*
the ENDURANCE *of* FAMILY

MINDY UHRLAUB

RIVER GROVE
BOOKS

Published by River Grove Books
Austin, TX
www.rivergrovebooks.com

Distributed by River Grove Books

Design and composition by Greenleaf Book Group
Cover design by Greenleaf Book Group
Cover image used under license from ©stock.adobe.com/anna

Publisher's Cataloging-in-Publication data is available.

Print ISBN: 978-1-63299-982-5

eBook ISBN: 978-1-63299-983-2

First Edition

To Dadder, David Weinberg,
and my brudder, Brian Weinberg.

And for Kirk, Ethan, and Alex.
You are my sun, moon, and stars.
This book would be nothing without you.

Contents

Somewhere in Utah

JUNE 2018. Kirk pulls our rental car up to the cluster of other SUVs at the specified Bureau of Land Management coordinates. Dust curls around our windows as we come to a stop. We lost our radio signal a long time ago, so we spent the bumpy dirt-road drive speculating on what we'd go through on our first and only visit with our troubled fourteen-year-old son, Ethan. Will he be angry with us? Is he healthy? Is he making progress? Did he start a fire without a match yet?

We've followed the rules and not brought any contraband, like games, cash, snacks, gifts, or promises. Before I open the door to the oven-hot air outside, I hold a deep breath and tell myself to make these five hours count. As the dust clears, I take in the environment that has been our son's home for the last four weeks. Juniper bushes and agave plants dot the arid rust-and-beige landscape. Jagged purple-black mountains jut diagonally in the distance. The car's dashboard says it's already ninety degrees outside, and it's only eight a.m.

High above the makeshift parking lot, a turkey vulture wiggles against the jet stream as it circles overhead. *Is it waiting for someone to die out here?*

Lean-tos have been erected in anticipation of parents' visits. We can't see Ethan yet because the therapists have asked the boys to set up their individual tents out of earshot of each other. As we open our doors, Ethan's therapist, Greg, a skeletal Mormon with several of his own sons, saunters up. He wears a floppy sunhat but still squints against the dazzling desert light. He holds the door open for me and asks if we brought anything. My throat is already so dry that I can barely croak out, "Just our hats."

Kirk grew up in this kind of weather and he seems comfortable against the sandy terrain. He's a tall, strong cowboy, and as natural as he looks in his hiking boots, cargo shorts, wicking tee, and baseball cap, he's unable to conceal the twitch on one side of his mouth when he smiles. I'm not sure if he's nervous to see Ethan or if he's trying to control the pain in his bones.

A teenage boy in khaki who looks several years older than Ethan struts past us with a hand-crafted bullroarer. It looks like nothing more than a piece of wood attached to a string, and he swings it overhead. He twirls it proudly as he leads his own mystified parents to his tent. The sound it makes is like a growling mountain lion. It echoes off the nearby cliffs.

Greg tells us that our son's bullroarer and backpack projects went well but that Ethan, the youngest in the group, has really struggled with starting the fire without a match—called busting coals. These are some of the wilderness survival milestones he'll have to accomplish before he can come home. Making fire with a stick, a bow, kindling, and a piece of twine has been the hardest.

I think back on other milestones that Ethan struggled with. Although, at the tender age of two, he was verbally gifted and could name each of the fifty-two birds on our Audubon playing cards, he rarely showed any interest in doing anything his parents asked him to do. When I begged him to sit on the potty, he refused. When it came to toilet training, no amount of cajoling or bribing worked. Promises of ice cream treats, M&Ms, stickers, or new toys were met with, "*No!*"

When the other moms in the playgroup had bragged that a single M&M did the trick for potty training their own toddlers, I kept quiet. Just that morning, when I'd asked Ethan to poop on the toilet, he had thrown the potty seat at me.

His lean-to is pinned to the ground with a large rock on one side and tied to a tall juniper on the other. Ethan emerges, wearing the same standard-issue khaki that the other boys do. Our son unfolds himself, and I'm stunned at how tall and skinny he is. His ribs poke out under the khaki shirt that hangs on his frame.

We grab him in a group hug as Greg takes pictures of us from a short distance away. Ethan's hair is a nest of long, tangled curls, and he smells as if he hasn't showered in the four weeks since he's been gone. When he pulls away from us, tears have made clean marks down his dusty cheeks. His ice-blue eyes twinkle against the accumulated brown grit on his skin.

"I'm so glad you could come, Dad," Ethan says.

"Me too, Buddy. It's good to see you."

I pat Ethan's sweaty back and dust floats from his shirt. I'm nervous that Ethan will beg to come home now that he knows that Kirk's chemotherapy will start next week. We've been briefed by Greg that Ethan handled the news of Kirk's lymphoma in a very vulnerable and open way. There were lots of tears last week, and the other boys were empathetic and helped him talk through his feelings during group therapy. I'm surprised that he only cries for a minute now and quickly brightens.

"Want to see my stuff?" Ethan asks. He ducks into his lean-to. Kirk and I shrug at each other and peer in. Just like at home, his belongings are neatly arranged. Two two-liter water bottles are propped up next to his collection of recently found bullet shells. A change of khakis, a pair of sandals, a tiny ration of trail mix, and a bedroll is everything he has, aside from the handmade backpack, which leans against the other side of his juniper outside.

"Wow!" is all I can manage as I look at his meager belongings. I have so many questions, but mostly I'm praying that all of this barren landscape and spartan nomadic lifestyle is working to change his behavior at home. I'd gotten accustomed to his disrespect over the years. It's hard to imagine him telling his trip leaders, "Fuck you" when he's being offered breakfast out in the open desert. I wonder if and what he's been eating and ask, "What was for breakfast today?"

"We learned how to make bread out of flour and water. I also had some raisins," he says simply, as if making bread each morning with Gila monsters at his feet were the most natural thing ever. Then he explains that because they don't get many fruits or vegetables, he got so constipated last week that he didn't move his bowels for four days. I don't have a chance to ask what the therapists did for him when he was so backed up. Ethan's already on to the next thing.

He steps back into the harsh sunlight and reaches into his pocket. He pulls out a bullroarer, like the one the other boy had. Ethan's doesn't look like much either—a palm-sized piece of wood shaped like a surfboard attached to a string. He's etched little designs on it, and it seems like it may be a work in progress. Ethan wraps the twine between his fingers and spins the instrument over his head in circles. It sounds like a motorcycle revving up. I'm so impressed that he's had the fortitude to be so industrious and creative out in the sand. Kirk and I both applaud. Then he tells us he had some success busting coals last night. He's been practicing so he can show us.

We follow him to a clearing away from any foliage or tents. In another pocket, Ethan has a bow drill set: a piece of wood a little thicker than a ruler with a little notch in it, a tiny bow made from string and a stick, a second stick, and some kindling that looks like hay. He leads us to a spot under an outcropping of rock, away from any wind, and he gets to work. He sets the notched ruler down and puts a tiny bit of kindling under the notch. Then he puts his boot on the end of the ruler, places the end of the bow into the same notch, and runs the second stick back and forth. As he does this, I remember what Greg told us on the phone before we came for a visit, "Your time together will be about three-quarters wonderful and one-quarter suck."

Ethan grunts with the effort, but the notch and the bow don't fit together very well. There's no sign of smoke, ash, or fire. He stands and stretches his back, reties his boots, and tells us he's going to try again.

"Good job. You'll get it," says Kirk. Ethan sighs and crouches down. Places a little kindling under the notch in the ruler. Puts the bow into the hole. Sets the stick against the string. Runs the second stick against the string. Back and forth. Back and forth. Nothing that resembles fire. Sweat pours from his forehead. He's panting after a few minutes.

"You can do it, Eth!" I tell him.

He turns on me and gasps, "No, I can't!" He throws the bow drill on the ground near my feet. Then he turns and stomps off to his lean-to. Kirk and I grab the components of his bow drill set and follow him back to the tent. He's face down inside, crying into his bedroll. I climb in and try to lie down next to him, but there's barely enough room for one person inside, and I don't want to knock over his shelter.

"I can't do anything right," he sobs. I pet his filthy hair. Tell him it's okay. That I love him. That I believe in him. Nothing from him resembles calming down. He cries for much more than a quarter of the suck time.

Kirk and I stand outside his tent and give him the space he needs to process his complicated and conflicting emotions of disappointment, excitement, love, self-loathing, and doubt. We need the time too. After living with our funny, brilliant, talented son for fourteen years, we made the agonizing choice to send him to a wilderness program. He was so volatile, angry, and disrespectful that our loving relationship with him had become one of open hostility. Kirk and I stare at each other, listening to our child sob in his tent. I feel like I can read Kirk's mind. *Was it the right choice for us to send him away?* I wonder. I don't have time to reassure myself because eventually, Ethan tires himself out and emerges from his lean-to.

We hug him again. For the first time, I notice a little string around his neck. At the end of it is an octagonal piece of wood with an etching of two open hands holding a heart. It's the wilderness program's pendant for the milestone for opening up to the group.

"What's that?" I ask, hoping he can acknowledge some of his accomplishments.

"The open heart. It basically means I cried in front of everyone," he says, wiping the tears away with the end of his giant shirt. Before we're ready to leave, Greg tells us it's time to go. We give our son one last hug and return to our blazing furnace of a rental car.

On the drive back to the hotel, the SUV feels like a clean and foreign environment, far away from the dust, frustration, heat, hunger, and starkness that is our older son's last summer before high school. We hardly say a word to each other.

Finally on paved road, as we exit a box canyon, we both jump when my phone rings. It's the babysitter, Arriel, asking if we got her texts and if we want to talk to Alex, our younger son.

"Absolutely!" I say. I put the call on speakerphone. We hear the sharp barking of our schnauzer-terrier mix, Dusty. We'd dropped them both at Arriel's ranch house because she couldn't leave her horses alone overnight.

"Hi, Mom!" Alex chirps. He tells us that he got to bottle-feed a baby goat and ride on the ATV at Arriel's. He tells us that he went swimming and that he helped Arriel make guacamole and adds, "Dusty peed on the drapes, but only after Arriel's dog, Rugby, did it first."

I find myself smiling at the thought of our son having so much fun. At twelve, he's already had some pretty tough things on his mind this summer. Nanee (his grandma) suffering with amyotrophic lateral sclerosis (ALS) and his brother going away are nothing compared to the upcoming chemotherapy that Kirk will have to start in July.

"How are you guys?" Alex asks us. He always seems to be concerned for others. Kirk tells him honestly that the visit with Ethan was both nice and very difficult.

"We can't wait to see you tomorrow!" Kirk says, but then we lose the connection in a twisting part of the road and the call gets dropped. By the time we get back to our hotel, we've received several pictures of Alex from Arriel, an email from the neuropsychologist who tested Ethan last month, and a voicemail from Dr. Sampson, the neurogeneticist I saw last week.

When I visited Dr. Sampson at Stanford, she wanted to know why I'd want to take the genetic test to find out if I carry the fatal mutation that causes the ALS that my mom has. There is no cure for ALS, and if I test positive for the C9orf72 repeat expansion, I'll likely develop the paralyzing disease too. Not only that, but if I test positive, insurance companies can deny me life insurance and long-term care insurance or drop me entirely from my health care plan. The crowning blow is that if I carry the C9orf72 mutation, our kids may carry it too.

After many months of watching my mom, Nanee, suffer losing the function in her foot and choking while eating, I've done lots of research. I know that science is the only way out of what ALS has in store for her. And I feel that the more doctors know about genetically inherited mutations like hers, the closer they'll get to finding a cure for ALS.

Doctor Sampson looked at me over her dark-framed glasses. I told her that I felt that there was a monster under my bed. That I could hear it scratching on my mattress. That it had red, glowing eyes and sharp claws.

"Most people would get a bigger bedspread and just hide under it. But I'm not that kind of person," I told her. She asked me what kind of person I was.

"The kind that flips the mattress over, grabs an Uzi, and blasts it to kingdom come."

She had my blood drawn and told me that if the test for the C9 mutation came back negative, she'd leave me a voicemail. And if it were positive, she'd want me to come in and talk to her.

The fact that there's a message from her on my voicemail gets my attention. After seeing Ethan in such a troubled state, I feel wrung out, and my husband's upcoming chemotherapy is like its own pending nightmare. I look over at Kirk, who is perched on the edge of the bed, already reading the results from Ethan's neuropsychological test on his laptop. His brow furrows, and he says, "Hmm. He's got a photographic memory and very slow processing speed . . ."

After five hours in the desert with Ethan, I need a minute to myself. I go into the bathroom to strip off my dusty clothes, shower, and clear my mind. When I blow my nose, my snot is rusty red with desert sand. I stand in front of the mirror looking at the new farmer's tan lines on my face, arms, and neck. Even though I'd used high-SPF sunscreen, I'm still glowing red from the desert sun. *I guess I can only protect myself so much*, I think. Wrapped in a towel, I listen to the voicemail. Doctor Sampson sounds terse.

"Mindy, I have your genetic test results. I need you to come in."

CHAPTER 1

Navigations

LATE JULY 2018. For my whole life—forty-eight years and counting—I've had a lousy sense of direction, but today I know exactly where I'm going. I'm so sure of my way that I bypass my GPS as I motor through the tree-lined suburb near Stanford University. I need to call my husband. I need to talk to Dadder. I've got to pick up Alex from theater camp. I need to feel him in my arms, to feel his heart beating against my own. I badly need a hug.

But first I must talk to my mother. I've called her Nanee for as long as I can remember. Mine was a family of nicknames.

"Call Nanee," I tell my car. As the words leave my lips, I wonder how to tell her the news the doctor delivered less than an hour before.

It takes my mother a while to pick up. She's in the middle stages of ALS, and getting around without tripping has become difficult. She wears AFOs—all-foot orthotics—so she can walk with help. I picture her wrestling her new walker to the dining room table, where the phone rests on a half-finished *New York Times* crossword puzzle. After six rings, she answers.

"Hi, Peep!"

I've had this unfortunate nickname since toddlerhood. When Nanee was potty training me, I'd run into the closet, close the door, and pee in my diaper. Princess Peepee was my nickname then. She's shortened it since.

Nanee also likes to share that I was so small that she had to make my clothes for kindergarten. Although no longer a toddler, her little Peep still wore a size 2T, which was way too juvenile for a five-year-old. Nanee bought patterns from the Sears catalog and sewed me big-girl clothes, like my favorite denim overalls with a big red apple appliquéd on the bib.

The hills along the northbound 280 corridor near San Mateo are already changed from kelly green to a jaundiced crackly yellow. The pavement ahead of me undulates in a superheated mirage. I hear the distinct fizz of Diet Pepsi as it's poured over ice in my mother's favorite NFL tumbler. It is uncomfortably humid in Naples, Florida, in July.

"What's wrong?" she asks, and I realize I haven't even said hello yet. I blurt it out because there's no other way.

"I'm positive for the C9 ALS gene."

Silence.

"Did you hear me, Nanee?"

She blows her nose. A longtime sufferer of allergies, she's never without a tissue.

"I'm so sorry, Peep. I didn't mean to do this to you," she sobs. I can't stand to hear her cry. She has a fatal disease, and my news just seems to make it worse for her.

"It's not your fault."

My mother blows her nose again. When I was conceived in 1968, scientists were still forty-three years from discovering the C9orf72 ALS gene. She had no way of knowing that she carried it. Until this moment she didn't know that she had passed it on to me.

"You have given me so much. Your sense of humor. Your love of language. Your long legs. This is just another thing," I say, trying to put on a brave face for her.

For once, she tries optimism. "You might not develop the symptoms."

She's right, though I've done my research. Of C9 carriers, only a tiny percent remain asymptomatic. I don't have the heart to recite statistics.

"You've also given me an opportunity. By knowing my genetic status, I can help find a cure. I can participate in clinical research," I say, trying to convince her that there is a silver lining in all of this.

"They've been looking for this cure for the last fifty years. It wasn't in time to save your grandpa Milton. It's too late for me—"

"You don't know that. Science is evolving fast."

I'm due to visit her. It's been two months since my last trip to Florida, and she's deteriorated a lot. Even though science is progressing, I know she won't live to see a cure.

I pass the San Francisco Airport, and we spend the next few minutes smoothing out the wrinkles in our conversation. I tell her I'm excited to see Alex tomorrow in Marin Shakespeare Company's *Pericles*. Nanee loves to hear about her grandkids. Any good news boosts her spirits these days. She says she's looking forward to her three-month move to Chicago for a round of Radicava infusions. She still holds out hope that this new drug may slow her suffering.

After thirty minutes, her speech begins to slur. Nanee's tongue and mouth get tired. It's the beginning of the bulbar onset phase of her ALS. I wonder if she should be enrolled in a voice-banking program in case she loses the ability to speak. I've heard that with eye-gaze technology, an ALS patient's recorded voice can help them to communicate. She's clearly too exhausted to hear about that now.

"Okay, I'm off to watch CNN. I love you," Nanee mumbles.

"I love you too."

The colorful stucco bungalows along Nineteenth Avenue give way to towering eucalyptus trees in Golden Gate Park. So many beautiful sights on a short, ninety-minute drive.

For months, I've been on the verge of panic for another reason. Last week, my husband Kirk started the first of several rounds of chemotherapy for an aggressive diffuse large B-cell lymphoma. Although his employer, an environmental consultation company, has been more than understanding and patient, I don't know if they realize he often spends the afternoon napping, when he's meant to be working from home. I hate to wake him up, but once Alex is home from Shakespeare camp, I won't be able to discuss this tough topic. Our son is only twelve, and he's already carrying the burden of his dad's cancer.

The road narrows as I enter a tunnel. It takes a second for my eyes to adjust to the dark, and then before I know it, I'm back out in the sunshine. The Golden Gate Bridge stretches its brick-red limbs across the bay. Tourists dressed in shorts and T-shirts cross the bridge, clutching their chests or their selfie sticks as they brave the incessant wind.

"Call Kirk," I tell my car.

He picks up on the first ring.

"Hello, Cute. What news?"

"How are you feeling?" I ask.

"Not as bad as I thought I would. I had a good nap," he says. I can hear birds chirping. He must feel good enough to be out in the backyard.

"That's great. So, my test for the C9 mutation came back positive—"

"But it doesn't mean you have ALS, right?"

Not yet, I do not say. Kirk's a cowboy. Literally. He was born and raised on Colorado's Western Slope. He had horses. And a cowboy hat. He's the kind of guy who, when given a cancer diagnosis, says, "No reason to panic until the doctor tells me to panic."

There's a 50 percent chance that I've passed a gene for a fatal neurodegenerative disease down to our sons, Ethan and Alex, but I try not to spiral into despair while on the phone. I need to pick up Alex soon, and I can't show up at play practice in tears. I exit the highway and head through the tony suburbs of Greenbrae, Kentfield, and Ross. It's hot in Marin, and Alex is lucky to be in the shaded auditorium at the Marin Art and Garden Center. As I pull into the parking lot, I say, "Well, there's no reason to worry unless the doctor tells me to."

Kirk, ever the optimist, says, "That's the spirit."

The lot is filling up with parents picking up their thespians. The crushing news about my genetic status feels like a boil on my ass; it only really bothers me when I sit with it the wrong way. And there are more immediate problems on my mind: my husband and mom with life-threatening illnesses. Not to mention our other son, Ethan, who is trekking with his therapeutic wilderness group across the Utah desert.

I've driven ninety minutes to end up here. I've navigated my first two conversations about the C9orf72 gene. I get out of the car and scurry across the hot parking lot. I need to feel the solid contentedness of my kid. The urgency of the moment pulls me through the gardens of roses and lavender that lead to the auditorium.

"Hi. Mom! I got my casting assignment!" Alex shouts. Holding his lunchbox, he jumps down from the stage, and I open my arms for a hug. He smells like childhood, like a prepubescent summertime boy. At twelve, he's already taller than I am, so I rest my head on his sweaty shoulder. I nuzzle his neck, where I see his pulse bumping up and down. In an instant, I feel like I'm home.

My own ALS battle will have to wait for another day.

CHAPTER 2

Sunset and Vine

I WAS THIRTY in the summer of 1999, and I'd just moved from Denver to Los Angeles to make a film whose screenplay I'd written for my thesis in graduate school. My coproducer, Joel, and I were walking from our office in Hollywood to our favorite Thai restaurant. Joel had terrible posture. Years of playing a kit in a drumline caused him to hunch over and practically drag his knuckles on the ground, like a gorilla. A tall, slim cyclist rode past us and said, "I'd recognize that walk anywhere."

He turned and pulled up on the sidewalk. He and Joel hugged and laughed about how they'd both relocated from Colorado to California in the last month. When Joel introduced us, Kirk, the lanky twenty-five-year-old cyclist, removed his helmet and biking gloves to shake my hand. There was something about Kirk that reminded me a little of a cowboy. He'd changed his horse for a bike, but when he removed his helmet, it was exactly like Clint Eastwood tipping his Stetson. He was a gentleman, and a handsome one at that.

I'd exited a five-year relationship in Denver six months earlier and was new to the dating scene in LA. Between getting settled in California and setting up a production office, I didn't have much time to suffer from loneliness. The few dates I'd been on in Denver hadn't materialized into second dates. The guy I'd been seeing for the past month in California recently told me he was dating someone else. I wasn't necessarily looking, but this Kirk was cute.

After a few minutes, Joel and Kirk exchanged phone numbers, and the cowboy rode off.

"I'm gonna marry that guy someday," I proclaimed. Joel looked at me and laughed.

Two months later, Joel was crewing up for a short film he'd written, and he asked me to be the script supervisor. I'd done some work in film and video during grad school, so being the scriptie for Joel's three-day shoot wasn't a big deal. It didn't bother me that it wasn't a paid job; as independent filmmakers, we often did freebies for each other.

I was delighted to learn that Kirk, the cycling cowboy, was going to be assistant director of Joel's short. Kirk and I flirted with each other on set, finding just about any excuse to talk to each other. He'd keep borrowing my pen. I'd ask him for the exact tape numbers when he'd already told them to me. At the wrap party, Kirk and I talked about how many times we'd been in the same place in Denver. The coincidences were too great to ignore. He'd worked for the Creative

Film Group. I'd worked for Women in Film. The two groups had put on a film festival in Denver together, and Kirk and I had both been there. Joel and I had thrown a grand opening party for my production company in Denver, and Kirk had been there (in the same room) the whole night. Kirk's brother played in a band in a club where I used to hang out in Denver, and Kirk was probably there too. We'd never met until the week Kirk moved to Los Angeles. It was almost as if we didn't meet until we needed to.

"I don't miss Denver, but I miss access to good hiking," I told Kirk at the wrap party.

"I miss hiking too," he said. He'd been raised in western Colorado, near the Colorado National Monument and not far from Moab, a hiker's paradise. We exchanged numbers, with the promise that we'd go hiking as soon as possible. He called me the next week, and we drove out to Malibu together.

I marveled at how comfortable he was in nature. Kirk always knew where he was going, which path to take, and how long it would take us to get to the next bend in the trail. He told me about his mountaineering trips to South America and about his adventures growing up with horses on the Western Slope of the Rockies. I listened attentively when he said that although he had three brothers, he was raised as an only child. His two half brothers were eighteen and twenty years older than he, and his full brother, Scottie, had Down syndrome and had been adopted by a woman who had other Down syndrome children. Kirk was used to spending time alone but also wanted meaningful relationships with new friends. He didn't know many people in Los Angeles, and he was eager to meet others.

His mother had recently died of colon cancer, and Kirk had managed his grief in the only way he knew how: to strike out on his own adventure. He spent three months traveling around Latin America completely alone. He'd previously gone to film school at the University of Colorado in Boulder. Once he'd processed the sadness of losing his mom, moving to Los Angeles was the realization of his dream to become a filmmaker.

I found it wildly sexy that Kirk had gone off on a three-month Latin American adventure on his own. Although I was outdoorsy and liked to travel, I could never imagine just dropping everything and going on an international road trip.

We ended our hike on the beach. Watching the sun set, we talked about what we both wanted to find in California.

"I've been working on this script for years. I want to be able to go to a theater, get some popcorn and Junior Mints, and watch my movie," I told him.

"Me too," he said. He'd already gotten several jobs as a production assistant on commercials. He was a fair distance away from being a filmmaker, but something told me that if he stuck with it, this gritty adventurer would succeed in anything he tried.

CHAPTER 3

A Bulldog for Others

LATE JULY 2018. Kirk lies flat on his back on a gurney in the emergency room at Marin General Hospital. I perch nervously on a plastic chair next to him, my hand shaking as I hold a barf bag that the physician's assistant handed me. The fluorescent lights and beeping monitor do nothing to distract us from the scruffy man in dirty clothes down the hall who's yelling, "Get your fucking hands off me!"

Kirk groans.

"Do you need to throw up again?" I ask.

"No. I just wish that guy would shut up."

I glance out the flimsy curtain into the hallway. It feels like we've been waiting forever for the red-haired nurse to return. A burly orderly pushes a shriveled old man in a wheelchair. A stooped old woman follows close behind them. The old man looks confused and asks his wife, "Did they put my glasses somewhere? I can't see."

She digs around in her purse and pulls out the glasses and says, "I have them, dear."

I feel a connection to this woman. *Am I going to be caring for my sick husband for the rest of my life?* I wonder. I text my friend Kristen, who has taken our twelve-year-old, Alex, for a daylong playdate with her son who's the same age. She was still in her pajamas when I dropped him off. I thank her for helping us in a pinch. Then I text my neighbor Cathy and ask if she'll walk our dog because I had to rush Kirk to the ER. Cathy texts back a thumbs-up. We're lucky to have a community that can circle the wagons when Kirk is so sick.

Something's gone horribly wrong with Kirk's cancer treatment. At first, everything seemed to be going as his oncologist, Dr. Lucas, said it would. He spent the morning getting his R-CHOP infusion at Marin Cancer Care. Because it was halfway through his chemo regimen, Dr. Lucas had ordered a lumbar puncture to determine whether the lymphoma had spread to his central nervous system. I'd walked him to the interventional radiology department for his spinal tap and waited until the radiologist gave me the word that it was safe to bring Kirk home.

Many people have a slight headache from the spinal tap. When the cerebrospinal fluid is removed from the central nervous system, sometimes its absence causes pain in the neck or head. Staying hydrated and lying down for a few hours after the procedure usually helps. The radiologist warned me to keep Kirk on his back until he was hydrated enough to stand without a spinal headache. Only Kirk didn't present any of the normal side effects of lumbar puncture. He drank plenty of water, but he didn't pee at all. Then he started feeling nauseous. In fact, he was so queasy that every time he raised his head off the bed, he threw up.

I spent a terrified night on the phone with the on-call oncologist. He told me that this was not a normal side effect of chemo. He referred me back to interventional radiology. The IR guy told me to call the oncologist again. The oncologist said Kirk needed a blood patch, a procedure to fix the leaking spinal fluid.

"The blood from the patient is injected back into the epidural area where the tap was. The blood will coagulate and form a patch over the leaking spinal fluid."

Only the IR guy wouldn't do a blood patch overnight unless Kirk was admitted through the emergency room. In fact, a daytime blood patch couldn't be scheduled with IR for thirty-six hours. If Kirk kept throwing up at this rate, he'd be dead within a day or two. I couldn't imagine my life without the man I love. My eyes filled with tears, frustrated that nobody seemed to care about him but me.

"You need to go to the hospital," I told Kirk.

"No hospital," he argued. I knew he hated hospitals. His mom had died of cancer after having surgeries to remove parts of her colon. Those traumatic memories probably made him fear hospitals. Moments later he said, "I feel like I'm going to die."

He was so skinny that if his head were not on his pillow, I wouldn't have known that there was anyone in our bed. I sat on the edge of the mattress, trying to distract him. I said, "It's not time to die. You haven't even made a bucket list."

I grabbed a notebook and started writing.

We came up with travel to Japan, Patagonia, and Alaska. Writing screenplays. Racing his old Miata on a racetrack, selling it, and trading it in for a new one. Eating nice food and drinking good wine with the family. A fishing cabin at the end of a dirt road, preferably in the mountains.

By morning, I was afraid for Kirk's life. My mind went to dark places. I thought about raising our two boys without him. I pictured burying Nanee and my husband in the same year.

Despite drinking gallons of water, he hadn't peed in two days. He was so violently ill that the smell of food cooking downstairs made him puke. And neither the IR nor the oncologist took responsibility for it.

"You need to go to the emergency room, Cute," I told Kirk again.

"No way. No hospital," he said. I'd been battling the health care system all night. There was no way I was battling Kirk, but the stubborn cowboy in him was starting to piss me off.

My hands, balled into fists, rested on my hips. "You have three choices: You stay here and die, I call an ambulance, or you be nice and get in my car. Right now."

I pulled over so he could throw up on the sidewalk, but we finally made it.

The IV bag that a red-haired nurse started for Kirk an hour ago has run empty. Kirk tries to sit up and groans again. The nurse finally returns with the on-call oncologist, who suggests we go home and wait it out. I look at her skeptically and tell her that she needs to see what happens when he stands up. The oncologist won't order the blood patch. In fact, she turns and walks out of the room. The IR doc won't schedule it either, but Kirk clearly cannot go home.

I go into what can only be described as bulldog mode. I jump to my feet to protect his life, driven by some prehistoric part of my brain, and I feel like a wife from the Stone Age. I feel a connection with wives back and back and back in time.

I turn to the red-haired nurse and bark at him to take Kirk on a walk past the nurses' station. If I can get the nurses to see how sick my husband is, he'll be admitted to IR through the emergency room. The nurse winks at me and says, "You got it, boss."

While they're out walking, I have a moment to myself. Amid the beeping monitors, the screaming disheveled man, and my vomiting husband, I think about all of the loved ones who are counting on me. The nurses in the hallway are asking Kirk, "Are you okay? You look a little green."

I think about the little old lady walking behind her husband and holding his glasses. As long as I'm here for him, everything will be okay.

The nurse returns with Kirk who does, indeed, look green. He winces as he's lowered back onto the gurney. The nurse reassures me, "He's off to IR for his blood patch."

Everyone should have a bulldog. Everyone should have someone to take care of them, but lately, it seems I'm caring for everyone else. And as I face my own health issues, I don't have a bulldog of my own.

CHAPTER 4

Square Corners

A MONTH LATER, I stretch the extra-long twin sheet over the mattress, wondering whether Ethan's feet will poke over the end of his new bed when he comes back. The wilderness therapist tells me that he's grown very tall over the last eight weeks, and the last thing I want when our son returns from the Utah desert is for him to be uncomfortable.

When I reach the end of the mattress, I unfurl the fluffy red blanket and tuck the end in tight, doubling it over in a square corner so he'll feel extra snug. I strip the dusty pillowcase off his pillow and wonder what he's been using to keep his head off the ground in his lean-to.

We've tried to keep his room exactly like he left it eight weeks ago, but there are some things we had to change. We've moved the airsoft BB gun from his closet to the garage. Now it's in a locked case up on a shelf. And as much as I hated myself for doing it, I riffled through his drawers of Legos when I noticed the edge of a $20 bill sticking out. It was a bill that I'd labeled with my initials, back when I suspected he'd been stealing from my purse.

There are other ways that the trust between Ethan and his family has eroded.

Toward the end of the previous school year, when Ethan was out of the house hanging out with his middle school friends and Alex was out chilling with his fifth-grade friends, I returned from the grocery store to find Kirk lying in the middle of the dining room floor, groaning. I dropped the bags and ran to him.

"What's wrong?" I asked.

"The usual. I have pain everywhere."

Dusty, our dog, was very attentive when Kirk was in pain. He rested his head on Kirk's chest and licked his face. Kirk had already endured six biopsies of six different bones. One biopsy included general anesthesia. The bone oncologist at the University of California, San Francisco (UCSF), cracked open his collarbone, pulled the marrow out, and ran the samples down to the lab. Kirk had spent a week with his arm in a sling, only to find out that nobody could tell what kind of cancer he had. We didn't yet have a name for the monster under Kirk's side of our bed. It did indeed have sharp teeth, big claws, and a taste for tall, thin cowboys.

I knelt on the floor next to him.

"I'm so sorry you're going through this," I said, rubbing his arm. "Can't you go back to your doctor and just insist on another scan?" I asked. And then, sitting there with him, I also wondered, *What if he dies? What if Nanee dies and he dies?* It was a grim thought to process, but I knew that I couldn't make them well. I struggled to compartmentalize my fears and focus on my suffering husband.

With all my attention on Kirk, it barely registered to me that our sons had returned together. Without even saying hello, they grabbed a basketball, explaining that they'd run into each other at the elementary school and were going to play a pickup game with all their buddies. Kirk shrugged and smiled.

"That was nice," Kirk said. He was always optimistic.

"Don't get excited. Someone will come home crying."

A minute later, Alex came home, screaming and holding his finger.

"You need to consequence him! He broke my hand!" he wailed. Kirk and I got up from the floor and held him in a group hug. His crying didn't get any quieter. I knew that being the younger brother of someone as angry as Ethan could be risky, but I wasn't prepared for what I saw. His finger, only having been injured moments ago, was turning purple. The tip of his digit stuck out at a weird angle.

"Oh, honey. We need to go to the hospital," I told him.

Kirk looked at Alex's hand.

"Don't touch it, Dad!" he whined.

"Let's get some ice on that. Mindy, can you get him an Advil?" Kirk asked. I stared at him. I was no doctor, but judging by the angle of his finger, I knew he needed an X-ray and a splint. Ethan came home, holding the basketball. He looked at Alex, whose hand was still in Kirk's.

"You're such a pussy, Alex," he sneered. I turned and marched up the stairs as Kirk laid into Ethan. I shook two Advil into my hand, and I could hear Ethan yelling back at Kirk, "So I kicked the ball out of his hand. I didn't mean to hurt him. Give me a break!"

The argument went on all night, Ethan insisting that it was okay to use your feet in basketball, and Kirk trying to extract an apology from him. At issue wasn't whether it was an accident; it was whether Ethan owned it. Alex muddled through the night, and the pain in his finger went away with Advil. *Maybe he'll be okay*, I thought. I was furious with Ethan for not being accountable for hurting his brother, but I was more upset at Kirk, who not only blew off his own health but was now ignoring Alex's.

The next day, the finger had swollen to the size of a kosher hot dog. I took Alex to the orthopedist, who took an X-ray and confirmed it was broken. My poor baby. I'd let Kirk convince me that he wasn't hurt when he really was. Every time I looked at the splint, I chastised myself for not advocating for him. When we got back from the doctor, Ethan looked up from the video he was watching and said, "So?"

"So, it's fractured," said Alex.

"But it's not broken," Ethan retorted. I explained that fractured meant broken.

"Huh. Well, I didn't do it," he quipped. I didn't know

whether it was an accident, but I knew he was responsible for it. I explained that Ethan owed Alex an apology.

"Sorry," he barked, going back to his video.

"Ethan, that was not an apology. What are you sorry for?" I baited him.

He glared at me and said, "Alex shouldn't have put his hand down there in front of my foot."

The dismissive tone in Ethan's voice spoke volumes. He really didn't care that he'd broken part of his little brother's body.

And that's how Ethan proved to me that he could not live with our family anymore.

I worry about telling anyone about Ethan's learning differences or temper. I don't want him to be perceived, or for him to perceive himself, as handicapped. Since birth, he's been angry. I worked in day care centers for years, and I never knew a child who cried more than my own son. He was verbally gifted. By kindergarten, Ethan not only could read several grades above his own but could also tell me to fuck off in ten different ways. I never knew why, even at a young age, he was so angry. I struggled to understand my unhappy boy, but in the end, the only thing I was sure of was that I loved him.

The pediatrician suspected that Ethan had ADHD, and we'd been taking him to a psychiatrist for several years, focusing on his anger management. I was mortified when, in fourth grade, he'd given his teacher the finger and thrown clothespins across the room in anger at other students. Enforcing rules around him was nearly impossible, as there was lots of pushback and little respect for parents. He lacked empathy and often bullied his little brother, Alex. Eventually, his psychiatrist put Eth on Intuniv, a repurposed blood pressure medication used to help him control himself. But he still had trouble focusing at school and was easily distracted.

I always suspected that there was something going on with Ethan that had nothing to do with inattention. He was whip-smart and could describe things in tiny detail, like how many people were wearing yellow or how many people were wearing blue jeans with red shirts in a crowded airport terminal. He could take apart and fix just about any gadget or machine that was broken. That said, when anyone tried to interrupt him during the construction of a Lego project, he'd explode in a tantrum, even when he was twelve or thirteen. It was so confusing and seemed like he was a two-year-old in a teenager's body. And he was taller than me by the time he was twelve, so when he got angry and lost his temper, sometimes I got scared.

Living in a house with a gifted, angry, tall, articulate child stirred up so many emotions for me. I simultaneously loved Ethan and was terrified of him. I knew my son, but I didn't understand him. I questioned my ability to parent someone so troubled.

I felt that whatever this thing was, it wasn't learned. We'd parented both of our children the same way, and Alex didn't have tantrums. Ethan was just programmed differently. It was his nature to take up the air in the room and be difficult. But by the time he hit middle school, Ethan had begun to break bigger rules, like the law that requires a child to attend school. He frequently was late to class, overslept and missed the bus, or walked out of classes he didn't like. I got emails and calls from the teacher, the principal, and the guidance counselor. Ethan was misbehaving. Ethan ditched class with his friends. Ethan is getting a D. Ethan needs an accommodation.

Ethan finished middle school with grades all over the map: an A in digital design to a D in math. By then, Kirk and I had already signed him up for the wilderness program, and he was to leave two days after school ended. If he was lucky, he'd be able to start high school on time.

As much as I want Ethan to come home, I can't picture him showing empathy for anyone, especially Kirk, who so clearly needs it now. I lie down on Ethan's newly made bed and shove the pillow under my head. What will he think when he sees Kirk without any hair? How will he react to Alex's theater successes over the summer? There are some things that will be so different for him when he comes home.

I start to cry when I realize I'm not ready to live with my firstborn son again. I pull the tightly tucked edges of the blanket from under the mattress, climb under, and hide.

CHAPTER 5

Happy

2009 TO 2015. It's hard for me to remember an extended time when the four of us were all happy being together. It seems like between cancer, ALS, Ethan's issues, the kids fighting, and the stress caused by the same issues, there has never been a time when we felt peaceful as a family, especially at home. Generally, we can put our differences aside when traveling or out in nature. Kirk worked for thirteen years as a trip coordinator for a high-end adventure travel company, and our family was the guinea pig for many kid-friendly trips abroad. The company would send us on international adventures on their dime. An early voyage was to the Galápagos Islands. I can recall seven-year-old Ethan and five-year-old Alex making friends with Galápagos giant tortoises in the arid rainforest near the beach. The majesty of the gentle, prehistoric reptiles was enough to quiet even the most agitated of us.

Then there was Kenya, when we took ten-year-old Ethan and eight-year-old Alex and stayed in Giraffe Manor with actual giraffes who stuck their heads through the windows of the restaurant. On that same trip, we went on safari to view migrating zebras and wildebeests as they crossed the perilous alligator-infested river. We saw a cheetah on the hunt and several lion prides that included adorable cubs. At night, we camped in safari tents after eating like kings in the mess hall. It was difficult to be unhappy on trips when nature took your breath away.

When the kids were twelve and ten, we cruised around Indonesia on a private yacht, and after a day of watching Komodo dragons in their natural habitat, we relaxed on the top deck, reading good books. I looked around at my contented family lying in the shade of the sails. We were all sprawled out on sun-warmed towels in our bathing suits and sunglasses, and I realized that it had been a few days since the last power struggle.

We also could get that vacation vibe just by hiking in our own town. By the time the boys were toddlers, Kirk and I would take them hiking in the hills above our northern California county. We'd drive to a trailhead, and once our boots hit the trail, there was seldom any tension. Kirk and I would load our backpacks with snacks and drinks, and as long as everyone was well-noshed, we'd all be happy. No ticks, rain, heat, dust, or tough terrain would bother us. In fact, it was usually on these hikes when we had the best conversations with our kids. With Kirk as our fearless tour guide, we were a symbiotic team.

There was one destination in particular that the kids loved: the rock fort. About a ten-minute drive from our home is an open space with several gradual hills. Many of the trails on the foothills lead to a shaded area with a natural rock formation that loosely resembles a house. Four walls and a roof have formed over the years. Somebody even tied a swing to an overhanging branch near the fort. When they were little, Alex and Ethan would beg to go to the rock fort, and Kirk and I would chase them up the hills, through golden waist-high grass, racing to see who could get to the fort first. After hours of climbing on the rocks and swinging on the rope swing, we'd run back down to the car, happy to have explored our natural environment.

The catch was that we'd always have to come home, and that's where we couldn't seem to be happy together. The close quarters were too much for Ethan, and to this day, he says that when the four of us are home together, he feels ganged up on. And this is problematic because, sometime soon, all four of us will live in the same house again. I can't imagine how Ethan will feel when he's back in our home where he feels so threatened.

CHAPTER 6

Protector of Humankind

AUGUST 2018. With Ethan away from home, Nanee suffering from ALS, and Kirk going through chemotherapy, Alex and I are like a two-legged stool. I wonder how someone as young as Alex can stay so positive. Right after the school year ended, he was in rehearsals for *Alice in Wonderland*, playing the demanding role of the Cheshire Cat. I felt it was important for him to participate in normal summertime activities, even if his home life was tumultuous, but I had no idea if he'd be up to it. He was only twelve, and he was extremely sensitive. But every day he woke up early, made his lunch, and went off to play practice. It was a welcome distraction. Not only that, but he'd memorized his lines without a problem.

By the time Ethan has spent eight weeks in the Utah desert, Alex has performed in three plays, gone to weekly guitar lessons, attended tennis camp for two weeks, and come home smiling every day. As contented as Alex seems, the stress of living with his father's cancer is wearing on him. He's peeled the skin off the tips of two fingers. He also has frequent nightmares.

It's a daily slog for all of us, Kirk especially, of course. Three times during his cancer treatment, he goes in for a high-dose infusion of methotrexate, which is meant to stop the growth of the cancer cells. As part of the R-CHOP chemotherapy protocol, it protects Kirk's central nervous system from cancer. It's so toxic that the nurses who administer it wear hazmat suits. They also wear thick gloves when they flush the toilet that he pees into.

High-dose methotrexate infusions require overnight stays in the controlled environment of the hospital. Because methotrexate is so poisonous, nurses have to watch for adverse reactions, and the hospital is the only place where the antidote is on hand.

Hospital food is disgusting. Kirk, being a foodie, requests that I bring meals from the outside. He also wants real coffee, so for breakfast I'm there. After Alex and I eat, I drop him at camp, race to a café, grab Kirk a scone and a large black coffee, and drive fifteen minutes to the hospital. Sometimes I bring him dinner and stay late into the evening. I'm happy to do it, but that means leaving twelve-year-old Alex alone for long stretches of time, which I don't want to do. Given the stress he's enduring, I feel it's unfair to leave him feeling unsupported at home. It's impossible for me to be there for everyone. I find myself asking people to stay overnight with Alex, and it is taking a toll on him. He needs me, and he needs his dad, and despite Ethan's unfair treatment of Alex, he actually misses his older brother.

One night we go on a walk with Dusty, and Alex starts bawling. I throw my arms around him and rub his back. He's usually such a happy kid. This is new.

"I have the hardest life of any kid I know!" he sobs into my chest.

He's not wrong, but I try to get him to put it in perspective. Daddy's going to be okay. Ethan will be okay. I'll always be there for him. But I honestly don't know if I'm telling him the truth. I don't know if Ethan will come home from the wilderness as a peaceful member of the family any more than I know if Kirk will live. Eth may never live harmoniously with us. Kirk could die. I try telling him about my own twelfth year.

"If it makes you feel any better, I understand. I had a very shitty twelve too," I say. He looks at me skeptically, wiping his nose on the collar of his shirt. I've always kept the topic of my childhood from our kids, as I don't want it to interfere with my parents' relationship with their grandkids. I don't want this conversation to be all about me, but I tell him the story anyway.

"Do you know why Papa and Nanee got divorced?" I ask.

"No," he says.

"Papa had an affair with another woman when I was your age," I say.

"You mean he had a girlfriend that wasn't Nanee?" he asks, intrigued. I don't really know how I found out that my dad was cheating on my mom, so I tell him what I remember. "Nanee was heartbroken. The trust between my parents had been destroyed," I say, knowing I'm revealing something that may make my dad look bad. I've always painted Dadder as a benevolent patriarch. I've never told my kids about his indiscretions, but once I start talking, I can't stop.

I remember Nanee sitting at the kitchen table and taking the hand of each of her kids. She reassured us that she, Brian, and I were a family. That Dadder still loved us, even if he'd had an affair with someone else. I also remember that my parents' divorce took many long months, and during those long months, Nanee referred to my dad as "The Asshole." It was confusing for us because after their initial separation, sometimes Dadder would move back in.

Eventually, they separated for good. After months of shuttling back and forth between my dad's apartment and our mom's house, I began to think about my parents' relationship. It didn't add up. My dad, who had protectively held the back of my bicycle seat when I learned to ride without training wheels. My dad, who used a garden hose to save our house from the flames in the vacant lot next door. He put his own needs over our family? He had sex with some woman who wasn't my mother? Why did he make her so mad? Back then, it may not have occurred to me that this was shitty. When I was twelve, I only knew that my father was flawed and my family was falling apart.

Talking to Alex this way has made me remember the premature end of my childhood innocence. It makes me hyperaware of the fierce love I have for Kirk. It makes me more protective of my kids' childhood and more aware that nothing will destroy our family.

"Parents screw up sometimes. My parents' divorce stole part of my childhood. But that doesn't mean Papa doesn't love me. And it doesn't mean he doesn't love you. Not only that, but I'm okay now."

Alex wipes the tears from his eyes and hugs me. He says, "I know. I'm so sorry that happened to you."

My little humanitarian. Here I am, trying to comfort him and let him know I understand how hard it is to be twelve. And he is comforting me. In the moment, we're both caregivers.

Sometimes I look up the meaning of people's names. Kirk means *church* in old English. In Hebrew, Ethan means *strong*. Alex (shortened from Alexander) means *protector of humankind*. When Alex was born, we banked his cord blood because Kirk was already a cancer survivor. As Ethan took his first wobbly steps, Kirk went through radiation treatments for MALT lymphoma in his stomach. The cord blood from Alex was our insurance that if Kirk ever needed a stem cell transplant, he could have the blood on hand. Without even knowing it, Alex was a protector of humankind from the day he was born.

We walk home in the dark. I'm holding Dusty's leash in one hand. My other arm is around Alex's waist. With his arm around me, I feel strong. Our two-legged stool might just stay upright.

CHAPTER 7

Gasket Heiress

1969 TO 1984. Watching Alex go through his complicated adolescence makes me reflect more on my own upbringing. Every year, on my birthday, Nanee tells me about the day I was born.

"It was a hot, sultry night in late August . . . ," she begins. My birth story always starts this way. I came into the world backward, feet first. My hip was dislocated. It was a painful beginning. The breech presentation of Nanee's firstborn must have been excruciating for her. Thank God I was only five pounds, thirteen ounces. I spent several months in a hip brace, but I still walked early, before I turned one. Nanee describes me as having been a precocious toddler, verbal and often prickly.

At a mommy-and-me ballet class when I was in preschool, Nanee told me to hold her hand and join the circle of other leotarded kids, to which I responded by sticking my tongue out at her. In front of all the other mommies. She was so mortified that she dragged me out of there and took me home. I can't say I blame her.

My earliest memory was when I was three or so. We lived on Dato Avenue in Highland Park, Illinois. Think John Hughes circa 1970 and you're close. Our kitchen, dining room, and living room made an excellent circular running track for a toddler, unless the kitchen door to the basement was open. I remember falling down the stairs when Dadder was halfway through tacking down carpet. His intentions were good; he was putting down padding in case I fell down the stairs. Unfortunately, he hadn't finished. I smacked my head pretty hard that day, and I can only imagine that it hurt him as much as it hurt me.

I also remember the day in 1974 when my baby brother, Brian, locked himself in the bathroom. Nanee and I shoved Saf-T-Pops lollipops under the door to keep him happy. By the time the Highland Park Fire Department picked the lock, Baby Brian had emptied Nanee's tampons and maxi pads all over the floor. He grinned at us through a rainbow-colored Saf-T-Pop mustache.

When I was five, my family moved from the Dato house to Lincoln Avenue South. We were a block from Lake Michigan's Rosewood Beach. Our new house was a grand colonial and on the same block where *Ordinary People* was filmed. *Weird Science* was shot in a neighbor's house a block away. Within a year, and with my aunt and uncle's help, my parents had enough money to build a tennis court in the backyard.

Brian and I had a unique relationship. He was bigger than me by the time I was six and he was four. One day, I was using my big mouth to tease him, and he pinned me against the built-in in the new family room. My pinky bent back and broke. I remember coming home from the hospital with a splint on my finger and Brian crying tears that wilted his long eyelashes. It was a formative moment for both of us. I learned to be kind to my bigger little brother. He learned to be gentle with his little big sister. It was the beginning of a close friendship that served us well during the rocky years ahead.

Nanee had taken several years off from her career as a high school Spanish teacher to raise us. I can recall her driving Brian and me the six blocks to school when it snowed. Chicago winters can be brutal, and although we were always outfitted with warm, layered clothes, she didn't want us to suffer through the bitter cold. She was a room parent at Ravinia School when we moved to Lincoln Avenue South. She was the one who cheered us on when we ran the fifty-yard dash on field day.

Dadder was in upper management at Fel-Pro, our family's business. The company, formerly Felt Products, had made horse blankets out of felt back in the early 1900s. When the automobile was invented, they turned to making felt gaskets for the internal combustion engine. My paternal great-grandfather had the foresight to nurture the proverbial golden goose, the one that laid golden eggs. By the 1950s, Fel-Pro was making the head gaskets for US Military vehicles, GM, Ford, Chevy, and John Deere. Nearly all of the men on Dadder's side of the family worked at Fel-Pro. My grandpa, who I called Bapoo; Dadder's brother-in-law, my uncle Denny; his first cousins, Ken and Paul; my brother, Brian; and my cousins Keith and Arthur all worked at the factory, and we all owned stock in the company. Trusts were created by my grandparents, and generations have benefitted from the generosity and hard work of our forebears. Dadder was always leaving early for work. He would wake up before dawn, do push-ups and sit-ups in the master bathroom, shower and shave, and leave before the sun came up.

During the summers, Brian and I would leave early with Dadder, who took us to Fel-Pro before breakfast. The company had incredible benefits for employees, including a day camp in Cary, Illinois, for employees' kids. Dadder's car would be chilly in the mornings, and the warm factory floor was a reassuring homecoming for us. The smell of rubber, the whir and clank of the assembly line, and the beep-beep of Felty, the automated train, made me feel like I was going through the gates of the Emerald City each morning.

Workers would shout out, "Hi, Dave!" as Dadder led us through the factory. Evelyn Evans, an elderly Black friend of Dadder's, would sometimes let me sit on her lap at her post in the packaging department. At a machine in the punch press department, another woman fitted gaskets onto a punch press that went *kaboom*.

I gawked at the protective gloves she wore and wondered how the machine's pull-aways automatically yanked her hands out so fast before the mechanical goliath could crush them. I didn't know then that there was a cable attached to a fly wheel in the thirty-two-ton press that activated the pull-aways.

We'd climb the stairs, and in the cafeteria, Dadder would sometimes buy me a slice of pound cake for my breakfast. Other days, I would get Lucky Charms and hot chocolate.

Triple-R (rest, relaxation, recreation) Day Camp was equally magical. In Highland Park, nearly everyone was Jewish and White. When I got on the camp bus each day, I went with the children of the factory workers who lived in other nearby towns. Chinese, Polish, African American, Mexican, Catholic, Hindu—whatever your origin, it didn't matter at camp. All employees' kids were campers. We all ate in the picnic grove, played capture the flag on the field, swam the two-hour junior lifeguard test in the pool, and played cards in the pavilion when it rained. We sang songs with the camp director, wove lanyards, stained our fingers purple on the mulberry tree, fought for the back seat of the bus, and chanted, "Hey, bus driver, speed up a little bit!"

Dadder's mother, Grandma Sylvia, must have had mixed emotions when it came to Fel-Pro. She saw her father build an empire, but she was never really a part of it. She didn't work in the factory and never spent the kind of time the rest of us did, getting to know the people who worked there. My grandma and I had a special relationship. She was an equal-opportunity teacher, and I was her eager student. At an early age, while I sat with her on her kitchen floor dying Easter eggs, she taught me about philanthropy by telling me stories of the refuseniks that she sponsored. They were Russian Jews who

were refused permission to emigrate to Israel. She taught me
that when you are born into a wealthy family, it is your responsibility to take care of others. Even though she wasn't active
in the day-to-day events at Fel-Pro, she spent years making
sure that the legacy her father created would benefit not only
the family and their employees but also worthy charities as
well. She created a trust for her children and grandchildren to
donate to NGOs.

Grandma Sylvia would invite us to swim in her basement
pool, carve pumpkins with her, and make pots with her on her
shaping wheel. While we treaded water, or scooped pump-
kin guts, or placed newly glazed pots in her kiln, she would
tell us about the League of Women Voters and the American
Jewish World Service. I have a vivid memory of going to
Grandma Sylvia's house one summer when I was about eight.
Dadder was picking up Grandpa's mail because Grandma
and Grandpa were separated. I'd never seen Grandma Sylvia
really mad, but she threw the stack of mail at my dad and
yelled, "Tell that asshole where he can put it," and it would
serve as another important lesson from my grandma: no relationship is permanent.

At Ravinia School, my best friends were Leslie Bailyn
and Chrissy Madden. We were all musicians: Chrissy and I
played the piano; Leslie played the flute. We had sleepover
parties at Chrissy's house and made chocolate chip cookies
and stayed up watching *Love Boat* and *Fantasy Island*. Rachel
Bennett moved in across the street. Their dog, Misha, was
always stealing tennis balls off our court, but despite growing

irritation between our families, Rachel was quickly accepted into our little gang. She played the violin, after all. We went to Shelton's for lunch, ordering hot dog specials from the ever-surly Shirley.

When we matriculated to Edgewood Junior High School, Joanne Nicholson and Pam Davidson joined our posse, to make our foursome six. We were a bunch of geeky musicians, all brainy in our own way. We would mourn the quiz we had to take on prepositional phrases as we waited in the long line for Chocolate Éclair bars at the Good Humor truck, which parked on the sports field every Wednesday.

Hebrew school was a prerequisite for Brian and me. Although my parents didn't have a Bar or Bat Mitzvah, I was pushed into my religious education. I started Hebrew school when I was nine and Sunday school even earlier. I was supposed to have donated my mom's spare change to *tzedakah* (charity) at Sunday school, but I spent it in the vending machine on Sprees, Twizzlers, and Butterfingers.

I was equally inadequate at other after-school activities. I had no proficiency for ice skating, ballet, or modern dance. During piano lessons, my sight-reading was undisciplined at best, but my musical ear was pretty great. I could hear a song once and sing it or play it on the piano, note for note, as far back as I can remember, and it served me well later in middle school chorus, where I never read the music but always sang it right.

When I was thirteen, I got my first job at Fel-Pro. I volunteered as a teacher's aide in the company's day care center. By then, I was too old for day camp, and some job training was in order. I closed the circle by working with kids like the ones who attended camp with me. Here were the children and younger siblings of some of my fellow campmates. I believe I was the first female family member in my generation to work in the family business. For three summers, I greeted the factory workers' kids, just as their parents and grandparents had greeted me on the factory floor. It just seemed right.

I had a good life: a beautiful home, parents and brother who adored me, after-school activities to keep me out of trouble, and great friends. But then it all started to fall apart.

CHAPTER 8

Query Tracker

AUGUST 2018. I just received another rejection from an agent who read the first fifteen pages of my debut novel, *Unnatural Resources.* I open my Excel spreadsheet and scroll down to her name. Next to the name is the number of pages I sent as an attachment to the email. Then the date when I sent the letter. The "Result" category is the toughest to stomach. Lots of "rejected" or "crickets."

I knew when I, a White woman in California, authored a novel set in the Democratic Republic of Congo (DRC), it might be a hard sell. I knew by telling the story of Black people, I might be accused of cultural appropriation. The DRC is a war-torn country with rampant violence and corruption, and my book's target audience is people with an expansive worldview and a conscience. It's not a light, beachy read; it's a two-hundred-page trek through the dangerous jungles of a developing African country. While *Unnatural Resources* is ultimately a story of redemption, it requires a certain kind of reader: one with a strong stomach and lots of empathy.

Clearly, agents are not known for their empathy. Or they don't have the patience to sell this kind of book.

I've sent letters of inquiry to more than 150 agents. My goal has always been to be rejected one hundred times before giving up on this book. I had no idea that only seventy agents would even get back to me, and 30 percent of those would want to read the whole manuscript. I've just begun to expand my search to include publishers because I desperately want to amass one hundred rejections and then give up on this novel. I've been working on it for seven years.

I first went to the Democratic Republic of Congo back in 2011. I'd read *King Leopold's Ghost* by Adam Hochschild, and it changed my life. The story read like a novel, painting the picture of Congo as a land rich in resources and plagued with White slavers, political instability, and grinding poverty. In 1885, when King Leopold of Belgium colonized Congo and stole resources, it was just the beginning of what lay ahead for the DRC's people. I was interested in this part of the world, and I started researching Congo's history. I read reports from Human Rights Watch and from V-Day, Eve Ensler's organization that seeks to end violence against women. What started with Leopold still continues in the DRC. To this day, rape, slavery, and corruption still exist there. It is because of the four hundred thousand women raped annually that I became interested in the DRC. I could never imagine having to live with the kind of terror girls in

Congo live with every day. The DRC is the rape capital of the world.

There is a small, vocal group of activists for women in Congo, and I quickly added my name to that list. In fact, I made it a mission to meet Adam Hochschild and tell him how much his book changed me. He lives in Berkeley, not far from me. We sat together one night at the *Mother Jones* fundraising dinner, where he told me that Eve Ensler was leading a delegation to the DRC to open a women's shelter there. The facility, City of Joy, was specifically for women who had survived sexual violence. Human Rights Watch was also putting together a trip to Congo to visit women and grassroots organizations who report gender-based violence. I'd already started drafting my novel in 2011 when I received my visa from the DRC's government.

When Ethan was seven and Alex was five, Kirk took off work and watched the kids. The trip was transformative for me. The DRC boasts giant volcanoes, deep forests, great lakes, endangered species, and some of the most joyful, beautiful women I've ever met. They dress in colorful wraps and headscarves with audacious prints that almost mimic the colors of the surrounding flowers. The smell of cookfires is ubiquitous, as is the cassava being cooked on them. You haven't been in rain until you've been caught in a storm in Goma. Congo is a lush, majestic country with strong, vibrant people. It is also so dangerous that I needed to travel in a large group with a security detail. Not only did I get to witness Eve's opening of City of Joy in Bukavu, but I was also able to take testimony of rape survivors and child soldiers. I traveled with Human Rights Watch into the countryside and spoke with women who had not only survived but prospered in the most dangerous place to be female. And that was just the first trip.

Two years later, I went back to see how the women at City of Joy were doing. Many had graduated from the program and were business owners, martial arts instructors, or on their way to law school.

On my second trip out to the jungle, I was sitting at a folding table in a makeshift lean-to. One teenage girl reached across the table, grabbed my hand, and said, "After hearing my story, you will cry your White people's tears, go home, and forget about me."

I am not going to forget about Congo. I'm not going to give up, and I'm determined to have this story see the light of day.

The cursor blinks under the category "Result," so I type "rejected."

I print out the latest spreadsheet for my query tracker. It's nine feet long. I've chosen a vocation based on rejection and heartbreak.

I recently visited Nanee in Chicago for her seventy-second birthday. She had moved from Naples, Florida, to her hometown to participate in a trial of a new drug, Radicava. I arrived in a rental car with a giant chocolate birthday cake with hot pink flowers on it in my passenger seat. Her partner, Jim, had met me at the door to their building in the city. To my surprise, he said that Dadder had found the ADA-accessible apartment for them.

I knew Dadder had contacted Nanee, but I had no idea he'd been so helpful to her. Nanee positioned her wheelchair at the door to their apartment. Even seated, she looked elegant. She had her contacts in, her inch-long nails recently painted a bright coral, and her roots dyed the same deep brown they'd always been.

"Hi, Peep! You telling her about Dave?" she asked Jim.

"Actually, he's been pretty great."

I stooped down and kissed her cheek. When she reached up to hug me, I noticed the large bruises on the back of her hand.

"What happened?" I asked.

"The veins on my arms collapsed, so now they do it in my hands."

It took me a minute to realize what this meant. If the doctors couldn't get Radicava into her veins, she wouldn't be able to stay on the drug that was supposedly keeping her ALS at bay. She'd already stipulated she didn't want a port or any other permanent attachment in her body. I knew she didn't want to prolong her suffering by giving up eating and installing a feeding tube. She wasn't the kind of person to go to therapy or try different prescriptions. There was no other way to administer Radicava, so her veins meant life or death for her. I was horrified, but I tried to keep the conversation light.

"Nice place," I said, taking in the wide hallways, the lower countertops, the extra-large doorways. There were no mats or rugs on the hardwood floors, and the bathrooms had grab bars and removable handheld showerheads. *This is what she needs in Naples*, I thought.

My father told me over lunch last week that he'd called her. He said, "So, I called Nanee."

What the what? Dadder and Nanee hadn't had more than half a dozen civil conversations since they'd gotten divorced in 1985.

"What did you guys talk about?" I asked.

"I told her the divorce was my fault. It wasn't her fault I had that affair."

I stared at him over our turkey sandwiches. In thirty-five years, Dadder had never taken responsibility for changing our family. He had gotten remarried to my stepmother, Jerry, more than twenty-five years ago. He seemed to have moved on in his life.

"I don't know what to say," I told him.

"You don't have to say anything. I just thought you should know."

He never had the same conversation with me or Brian. He never apologized to us. I only said, "I'm glad you did that."

I wondered whether she had been waiting for that apology for all those years.

"Better late than never, I guess," I told Nanee.

We pushed Nanee's chair down the street to a Greek restaurant and toasted to her over prosecco. While the saganaki flamed in its cast iron pan, I thought about how much grit and determination it took my mother to endure a bitter divorce, raise two kids on her own, start a business, find a happy relationship after her marriage fell apart, and fight for her life.

The women in my life have taught me lessons in tenacity. Getting my book into the world has been a grind. I return to California to the futility of querying agents. By the time I look at my nine-foot-long query tracker printout cascading down my wall, I don't even consider the possibility that *Unnatural Resources* won't get published. The rejections are nothing compared to real struggles. The girls and women in Congo don't give up when they are brutalized. Nanee doesn't give up when her veins collapse. There's no way I'm going to admit defeat just because agents don't like my book. Nanee didn't raise a quitter.

CHAPTER 9

Double Black Diamonds

AUGUST 2018. Ethan and I peruse the Utah memorabilia in the gift shops at the SLC airport. Ethan, obsessed with anything related to weaponry, flips through a *Guns & Ammo* magazine. The wilderness therapist told me to keep a close eye on him. He might backslide into violent behavior. He may run away or lash out at me. Is it a bad idea to let him even look at a magazine like that? Can I stop him if I want to? On a display hanger is a T-shirt with two black diamonds on the front, just like on a ski slope. Under the shapes it says, "Very Difficult," and I ponder buying it for Ethan, even though it would probably make him angry.

The issue of where Ethan will go to school when he returns from the wilderness has been weighing on my mind. Most kids who participate in wilderness therapy go straight to a therapeutic boarding school. Because Kirk is going through chemo, and because we want to have our family together, we insist on bringing him home and giving him a chance to be with us. Before I picked Ethan up from his eight-week wilderness program, I visited several therapeutic boarding schools in Utah and realized that if Ethan can't manage public school, that will be his next step.

His middle school grades are so bad that no self-respecting local private school will accept him. One therapeutic school in particular, set at the base of the Wasatch Mountains, has caught my eye. There are only thirty students and twice as many staff. It's owned and run by women, all of whom are mothers. Most importantly, the student body comprises boys who are very bright and behave badly. It's the ace in my pocket.

Ethan has not had any exposure to electronics in eight weeks. Even a movie on the plane is out of the question. We're not sure if the wilderness program was effective in breaking him of his screen addiction. Many kids fall back into old habits, like obsessive screen watching or video gaming once they've spent so much time in the wild. Many parents loosen the rules around "screen time" boundaries because they feel guilty about sending their kids away. I don't know how to keep him entertained on the plane home, so I buy him the magazine, a book of Mad Libs, and a bag of his favorite candy: cherry-flavored Swedish Fish.

Ethan being home is a huge adjustment for all of us. Used to living outside and hiking from campsite to campsite, he has to adjust back to living in a house and taking showers. He needs to follow different rules. Instead of making his own meals and carrying everything on his back, he'll have food prepared for him, fresh from the fridge. His school book bag will be the only thing he's got to carry. Things for him are further complicated by the fact that he'll have to explain to all his friends at home where he's been. The school mandates that each kid gets a district-issued tablet. Although we're trying to ease him back into electronics, he'll have the internet on his school iPad. He'll have to navigate the cyberworld that students live in, as well as the unfamiliar environment of high school. I feel for him and find myself hugging him and patting his back in passing. As hard as it is to live with Ethan, I've missed having him around.

"I love you, Ethie," I tell him daily. He leans from a foot taller than me to wrap me in his long arms. His ribs still poke out from under his shirt. I choke back tears when I hug him. As hard as he is to live with, I deeply believe our family needs to be together.

For us, we have to allow him to reintegrate into the home. Alex will have to cede the title of "only child" to "younger brother" again. He'll have to learn to stand up to Ethan and also give him space to be the older brother. Kirk and I, unused to disciplining a difficult kid all summer, will have to hold boundaries. We also have to give him the attention he deserves, without letting him hold the family hostage. It's our job to help him transition into high school.

Before bringing him home, we reached out to our local school, Drake High School, and put together an Individualized Education Program (IEP) plan for him with the resource department. I spoke with the assistant principal, and he assured me that he would keep an eye out for Ethan. We also hired two transition mentors for our son. One is a young lady named Yoshi, who used to work in a wilderness program and knows how to speak the language they use there. She understands the shellshock of kids trying to readjust to living at home. The other is a mentor named Phil Jones, a large, authoritative man who doesn't take any shit and puts the fear of God into kids who threaten to go astray. It is Phil's job to remind Ethan what will happen if he treats his family badly (therapeutic boarding school), breaks the rules (juvie), or breaks the law (jail).

Kirk and I put together a list of expectations for Ethan. It was a contract we made him sign to guarantee he'd follow the house rules.

Dear Ethan,

Congratulations on completing your Outback adventure! You've accomplished so much, and we're proud of you. We've missed you, and we really look forward to welcoming you back.

We all want home to be a peaceful place

where we learn and grow together. This requires some new arrangements between us, and also some new rules.

This next year is going to require hard work. All families have conflict. How we resolve ours will be the key to a peaceful home, and you will play a vital role in this process. As part of coming home, we ask that you agree to the following things.

EXPECTATIONS

- You will have an IEP (Individualized Education Program) in place at Drake as soon as possible.

- You will attend weekly therapy sessions with Dr. Schwartz.

- You will meet weekly with a wilderness-to-home transition mentor to help you adjust.

- You will participate in soccer or another physical activity year-round.

- You will maintain at least a B average in school and not skip any classes.

- You will participate in weekly family meetings in which we all reflect on how the family is doing.

RULES

- You will try not to yell or swear at your family.

- You will use "I feel" statements, like "I'm feeling frustrated," instead of "Fuck you."

- You will avoid unhealthy peer relationships, including any that involve illegal activities.

- You will not bring knives or other weapons to school.

- You will not make plans without your parents' consent.

- You will avoid unhealthy use of technology.

- Regarding your smartphone, we will activate the service in two months, provided that you are following the expectations and rules above. Technology is a privilege, and it can be taken away.

We think it is only fair that we make promises to you, too, as our part in this process. In addition to our love, support, and caring, we agree to do the following things.

- We will try not to yell at you when we are upset.

- We will try not to nag you or force you to talk when you'd prefer to be left alone.

- We will work to understand your feelings, and to help you understand ours.
- We will listen attentively to what you have to say.
- We will remain in therapy in an effort to work on ourselves and our parenting.
- We will try to trust you and give you independence where it is deserved.

We expect you will have moments where you regress to old behaviors, and we will too. What we're hoping for is clear, forward progress measured over days and weeks, not hours.

If we feel things have gone too far off track and the home environment is no longer effective, you may attend a therapeutic boarding school. If it came to that, we think you'd know it was time too.

We have faith that all the challenging work we do together will help create a happier family. Ultimately, the goal is to live peacefully together, support each other, and treat each other with the love and respect we all deserve.

We love you.

Mom & Dad

The transition back to school is difficult. Over the summer, Eth has had no contact with his friends who are starting the year with him. He has the advantage of knowing his buddies from middle school, but many of them are into sports that he doesn't play, and several of them have experimented with drugs over the summer.

Ethan has after-school activities every day: tutoring on Monday and Wednesday, Yoshi—the transition mentor—on Tuesday, Dr. Schwartz on Thursday, and soccer on Friday and Sunday. It's busy but manageable.

Ethan has developed an interest in art, so I go to the local art store, ten minutes from our house, and introduce myself to the cashier, Louis. It turns out he teaches a graffiti art class that is targeted for kids in trouble and at risk. He runs it out of a local pizza shop. When I meet Louis, I can't exactly picture his teaching style. Louis is a hip-looking, rough-and-tumble guy with lots of stubble, cigarette stains on his teeth, and an aura of having fallen on tough times. I don't want to judge him, but as cool as he seems, I think it's a little weird when he tells me that he mostly hangs with former gang members between fourteen and eighteen. Still, I know this is a reputable art store, and art may keep Ethan out of trouble. Plus, the fifteen-minute bike ride is good exercise.

Ethan obsessively accumulates markers, pens, journals, and canvases. It's good he has an artistic outlet, but the number of alcohol-based pens and markers make me nervous. Many kids sniff the alcohol in markers to get high, and though I've never known Ethan to do it, I wonder when he draws in his room with his door closed. Sometimes, I go to pick up Ethan from art class and he's not there. Sometimes, he and Louis go for walks in town and end up at a convenience store, a mile from where they met. One day, after texting Ethan from outside the pizza shop, I see them walking down the sidewalk toward the convenience store after class. I honk and pull over. Ethan high-fives Louis and gets in.

"Eth, I've been looking for you. If you're not going to be where I dropped you off, can you please text me and let me know?"

"Fair enough," he tells me. It's not really an answer or an apology, but at least he's civil.

One day, Alex tells us Ethan bragged that he inhaled a propellant from a CO_2 cartridge and got high. It gets our attention, but we don't want to out Alex as a narc, so we keep an eye on it but don't say anything to Ethan. One night, when we're at an event with Alex, Ethan, who is supposed to be home doing homework, jumps on his bike and rides the fifteen minutes into town "to find Louis."

Ethan has a talent for graffiti lettering, and Louis is responsible for teaching it to him. But I don't entirely trust Louis. And I don't trust Eth yet either. I'm nervous about all the time they spend together. Ethan, reticent to make any plans, wants to spend as much time with Louis as possible. Kirk and I are alarmed. We consult Dr. Schwartz, Ethan's psychiatrist. We all agree that Ethan is going down the wrong path and conclude his relationship with Louis is a problem. Kirk and I make a pact to tell him art lessons with Louis are over.

Sometimes, on the weekend, Eth goes on creek walks with two of his friends from high school. He takes off early in the day and sometimes does not return until dinnertime. With any other kids, I'd be thrilled that Ethan gets outside, away from the computer. But one day, in his room, he accidentally leaves a note on his desk. It lists:

- Sleeping bags: all
- Clothes: all
- Knife: me
- Lantern: me
- Rope: Chester
- Doinks: Jake
- Food: me
- Water: Chester

I consult *Urban Dictionary* for the word *doinks* and learn it's slang for joints. That afternoon, he asks me, "Can I spend the night at Chester's?"

"To be honest, Eth, I'm nervous about you going. What exactly will you be doing?" I ask. He has every opportunity to tell me the truth. I want to trust him.

"Come on! We've been friends since first grade! You know his parents!" is not exactly the answer I was looking for.

"I want to talk to Dad about this first. Let's wait until he gets home from the store," I start. He balls his hands into fists and grumbles, "You can't make any decisions without Dad."

He's right, but he's baiting me into caving in. I need to parent my difficult child, and it's almost impossible to do it effectively in the moment. I have a husband with cancer, a mom with ALS, and my own ALS genetic mutation to contend with. The pressure's on me, and I reach into my own heart and acknowledge I need to be strong for my son. For my family. I take a deep breath and stand my ground.

"If you want permission, you'll have to wait. I'm only one of your parents, and I want Dad to be on the same page as me."

I know if he's smoking pot, it's a direct violation of our contract, especially the rule: You will avoid unhealthy peer relationships, including any that involve illegal activities. The punishment for breaking the law is removal from the house to a therapeutic boarding school. He's only been home for three weeks. I don't want to have to confront him on it. I want to give him the benefit of the doubt. I talk to Kirk about it, and we agree to contact the host of the sleepover.

We text Chester's dad and warn him about keeping a close eye on the boys. They're potentially up to no good. Chester's dad is a hard ass. He's a martial arts instructor and parents with an iron fist. We allow Eth to go but make him promise to honor our contract, even when he's at someone else's house.

In the morning, Ethan returns, saying he had a wonderful time. We check in with Chester's dad, who says he'd caught the boys trying to sneak out during the night, but the rest of the sleepover went without incident.

Kirk and I breathe easier, knowing Ethan is staying out of trouble, for the moment. We clamp down on the computer and the camera with the knowledge they're temptations that Eth can't manage. We try to put aside the suspicion that he's doing drugs. His friends are basically good kids. Only he still can't manage to wake up for school. He's definitely doing something at night that he shouldn't be. One morning, when Ethan is especially bleary-eyed, I wait until he finally leaves for school and go on a mission to find the source of his sleep-lessness. Computers locked? Check. Phone disabled? Check. Xbox controllers away? Check. Camera confiscated? Check.

Then I go to the guest bedroom, which is downstairs, away from Ethan's room. I click on the television and see a young, surgically altered blonde girl getting gangbanged. The remote has been put on mute. The color rises to my cheeks. How could we have been so stupid?

With every breach of our contract with Ethan, the stress level in our home goes up. I feel like I can't trust him to use a computer. I stand over him when he does his homework to make sure he's on task. Kirk constantly checks his browsing history. I question him about where he goes and with whom. As Ethan puts it, I am "always up his ass."

Alex feels the strain too. He says he has pain in his knee. Then pain in his heel, then pain in his ankle. It seems to be attention-seeking pain, so we struggle to attend to Alex's needs as much as possible. But Ethan sucks the air out of our house. One afternoon Alex makes an elaborate LEGO structure, which spells out: I WANT TO DIE. The same day, I get a note from him that reads:

Dear Mom and Dad,

I love you so much, but I don't think I can live with Ethan much longer. I am tired of having to listen to you talking about his grades and fighting about his screens. I am sick of it, and I go to bed thinking about it each night.

Love,
Alex.

This breaks my heart. How can I reassure him, given I feel the same way? I ask him to please consider seeing someone who is impartial to talk about his feelings. He refuses to go to a therapist, but he loves his middle school guidance counselor. He reaches out to her, and they start meeting the next day.

His friend Casey is a reliable source of comfort for Alex. They're at an age when being boyfriend and girlfriend means riding bikes together each weekend. They also sing in the school chorus together, and when Casey comes over, they play duets on the piano. Sometimes I see them hugging or holding hands. She loves him and trusted him with her feelings when her parents went through a painful divorce the previous year. Sometimes she texts me saying she's worried about him. Although she's concerned, I can tell the more time he spends with her and with his other friends at school, Alex is improving. The more time he spends away from Ethan, the happier he seems. Even after a few weeks with the guidance counselor, Alex starts to open up to me about Ethan. He talks about Ethan's bad choices, about his unending fascination with breaking the rules, and about what he'd do if he were in Ethan's shoes. Alex is so busy outside of the house, with choral performances, school plays, and music lessons, he has very little exposure to his brother. I make every attempt to be there for all of Alex's practices, lessons, and performances. When there's a volunteer opportunity at school, I take it. Alex's sense of humor comes back. He starts to forget about every little ache and pain he has. He's sensitive, but he bounces back.

One day, I find this list in his room.

THINGS THAT MAKE ME HAPPY:

Acting, making music, playing music, writing, watching movies, hanging out with friends, biking, going on walks and hikes, playing with animals, spending time with family, celebrating special things, listening to music, eating food, receiving gifts, building and making things, making new friends, learning new things, helping others, being respected by others, being understood, loving and being loved, school.

Still, Alex seems to be able to find joy amid the chaos in our home. Kirk is weathering the cumulative effects of chemo and is able to find the energy to work from home, although he's greatly debilitated by having to monitor Ethan all the time. I find even though I am a natural at caretaking others, I'm letting my own medical issues go unaddressed. I've not told my kids anything about my genetic test or my own ALS diagnosis. In fact, I'm so nervous about putting undue stress on my kids that the only people I tell are Kirk, my brother, and my parents.

Carrying the lie-by-omission around is wearing on me. Watching Nanee die of ALS is wearing on me. Getting a positive test result for the C9 mutation makes me feel like I have no control over my own body. I feel like I'm standing in a low valley when a tsunami is approaching. I need to find a path to higher ground. And I'm convinced that science will show me that path.

CHAPTER 10

A Calling

WINTER 2018. I am determined to spend more time focusing on my own health. I enroll in a longitudinal study for C9orf72 at the ALS clinic at the University of California, San Francisco (UCSF). It's called ALLFTD because frontotemporal dementia and ALS both live on the same C9orf72 gene. For three days in a row, I drive into the city and submit to exams to determine my base levels of cognition, brain function, muscle fortitude. I sign up for a magnetic resonance imaging (MRI) to be done, even though I have paralyzing claustrophobia. I do an entire day of cognitive testing. I have a physical exam to assure I'm not showing signs of ALS yet (I'm not). I give countless vials of blood. Then I have a few hours of genetic counseling.

The head counselor urges me to recruit as many family members from my mom's side into the study as possible. If UCSF has a bigger population, they can study any symptoms of ALS or FTD progression over time.

Nanee's family is unilaterally opposed to knowing their own genetic status. Everyone besides me is unaware of whether they have the C9 mutation or not. I feel very alone in this fight against ALS. Sometimes I feel angry, depressed, and betrayed like I'm the only one in the family who cares. I understand that they're deathly afraid to know, but I sure could use an ally. And because my kids are minors, they're not allowed to know their genetic status. Alex and Ethan have already been through the trauma of seeing their dad almost die from cancer. There's no way I'm going to out myself to them as a C9 carrier.

As much of an ordeal as it is to submit to testing, I know I'm making an impact on ALS research. Instead of feeling sorry for myself, I'm empowered. ALS is a disease that takes everything from patients. While I'm still asymptomatic, I still have control over the disease, and I can make choices about how I give my body to research. UCSF has my genetic material, and they're going to use it in a CRISPR gene-editing study, to see if the C9 gene can be switched off. I'm proud to donate blood to innovative research that might ensure that my kids—and maybe I—won't die of ALS.

All of the online research I've done about familial ALS shows a bleak future for genetic carriers like me. There is no cure for ALS. Presymptomatic carriers of genes like C9orf72 are not put on ALS drugs. We're not enrolled in clinical drug trials. In fact, we're not even considered patients. There's no standard of care for people like me. I will fall through the cracks, and so might my kids. It dawns on me that if I had high cholesterol, my doctor would help me with a nutritional plan. She'd put me on cholesterol-lowering medication so that I could prevent having a heart attack or stroke. Why is there no way to prophylactically prevent genetic ALS?

I realize I have a calling. Not just to help cure ALS, but to write about it, too. It's a big thing for me to acknowledge I'm going into battle against the unseen monster of my own ALS. Kirk has finished chemo with few lingering side effects. With Kirk feeling stronger, the two of us can be there to support Ethan and Alex. Kirk can be there to better support me. I can picture a future for myself where I don't have to worry about Kirk's health. A future where I don't have to worry about Ethan going off the rails. A future where I won't have ALS.

Kirk and I had promised ourselves that if he was still alive, we'd treat our family to an international trip. While we've experienced our share of rotten health luck, we recognize that we're a lucky family, and Kirk plans a trip for all four of us to Granada. We stay at a tiny, all-inclusive resort, where lovely, warm-hearted staff bring us high tea and cookies at four o'clock on our own balcony. Our duplex-style casita steps directly onto the white, sandy beach. Because his birthday is December 27, we celebrate his wellness, his birthday, Christmas, and New Year's all on one trip.

We take a tour of a chocolate plantation one day. We play tennis on hot, steamy, clay courts. We go out to seafood dinners. We hike to the locals' beach for a day trip. But mostly, we sit in the sun and play in the healing Caribbean waters. Our most difficult decision each day is whether to lie in the sun on the beach or lie in the sun at the pool.

On New Year's Eve, we lie on our backs on the warm sand and marvel at the fireworks being shot over our heads out to sea. My hands are behind my head, and Alex's head rests on my elbow. His tears run onto my arm as he sobs, "We made it," and in seconds, we're all crying. We've lived through Kirk's cancer, Ethan's wilderness experience, Nanee's ALS diagnosis, and here we are, lying on our backs in paradise.

On our way home, we visit Nanee and Jimmy in their condo in Florida. She's much weaker than the last time we saw her. The walker is becoming too difficult for her, but she insists on using it anyway. It takes three of us to get her out to the pool, and even then, she can't move from her lounge chair. The days of her getting into the pool, even with help, are over.

Kirk's hair has started to grow back, sort of. His thick, tan curls are replaced by a fine, blond peach fuzz, like a baby's. Nanee lectures him to wear a hat, and when she feels like she's made her point, she harps on Jimmy, who is limping from a recent back surgery, to also wear a hat. Cranky, Jim snaps at her. It's clear that living with someone with needs as great as hers is beginning to wear on him.

Jimmy and I take a walk on the beach one day. He tells me, "Nanee is really having trouble. When I go to Virginia to check on the business, she accuses me of abandoning her."

I've been there when she accuses him of being unfair to her. Sometimes she gets fatalistic. She goes to dark places, talking about how she wants to hasten her death. Sometimes she threatens to throw herself over the balcony. Sometimes she says she'll drown herself in the pool. It's painful for me to hear it. It can't be easy for Jim to live with someone who expresses how hard it is to live with ALS.

"I love her, but I can only take care of her to a certain point; I'm not willing to change her diapers when it comes to that."

Brian and I had this conversation a year ago. What will happen when Jim can no longer take care of her anymore? Florida isn't a state where people can legally get a doctor or medical practitioner to help them end their life. Given the number of old people living with terminal illnesses in Florida, it baffles Jim that she can't make any sane end-of-life plans. He asks me to help her look for places to live when it gets too hard for her to live in their home.

When we leave, the kids make me explain why I'm crying on the way to the airport.

"She won't let me cry in front of her," I say. I struggle with letting her be the agent of her own life. I think back to the times when she had to give up control of me: when I went away to college and joined a band, when I decided to have a limited guest list at my wedding, when Kirk and I made the choice not to send our kids to Hebrew school, raise them to be practicing Jews, or throw Bar Mitzvahs for our sons.

And then I think of a time when she stepped in and took over for me. It was when Ethan was born.

Nanee had flown in to stay with us for Ethan's birth. I labored with my firstborn for more than thirty hours because the hospital wouldn't admit me. My cervix wouldn't dilate on its own, and because I wasn't progressing, the nurse didn't want to check me in. By the tenth hour, my contractions were less than two minutes apart even though I wasn't dilated, and I couldn't eat because I kept throwing up. By the time I could push, I was too exhausted and dehydrated to deliver Ethan normally. They called the neonatal intensive care unit (NICU) crash cart team into the delivery room. He was delivered vaginally with forceps and was unconscious. His APGAR scores were low.

After several weeks, Nanee wrote a scathing letter to the head of the OB-GYN department at California Pacific Medical Center about the torture they put me through. She said their treatment of me was inhumane. I was too out of my head with postpartum depression at the time to thank her. She didn't want to see her baby suffer any more than I wanted to see mine suffer. Ultimately, that's what good parents do: stand up for their kids when they're suffering.

What is my role as a daughter, now that Nanee is suffering? Is it my job to tell her what she needs? Is it my duty to step in and take over for Jim? Or is it my job to let her live, and die, the way she wants to?

There are no easy answers.

CHAPTER 11

Voyages

EARLY 2019. It's Valentine's Day, and like two kids on a first date, Kirk and I giggle at the prospect of a cancer-free weekend away. I've rented a cabin up the coast, where all our meals will be delivered and we can curl up in front of a fire. The rains have come back to northern California, and we drive through the drizzly fog to our getaway. We've left Ethan and Alex with Michelle, a sitter who is one of their favorite adults. She's about the same age as we are, but she has an easygoing spaciness both of our kids like. When we arrive at our cabin, I pull out a bottle of champagne and the Write On Mamas new anthology, *She's Got This!*, where my essay called "The Oak Tree" appears. Although it isn't the publication of my Congo book, it still feels like a writing success. The pieces are well-curated, and they fit together to make a stunning book. I'm proud to be part of the sixty-woman group, the Write On Mamas, and Kirk and I toast to success—mine and his.

When we return home, Michelle is packing her things. She reports the boys are getting along so well that she let them go out hiking without her.

"In this weather?" I ask, gesturing to the drizzle out the window.

"I know. But they wanted to go, so I thought it was okay," Michelle says. She also reports the weekend was uneventful. Alex went to his music lesson. Eth won his indoor soccer game. The dog got walked and fed. We pay her and send her home. It isn't long before Eth returns, soggy, winded, and full of criticism about Alex.

"Alex is such a wuss. He couldn't even keep up with me when I told him to jump the river!" He kicks off his drenched shoes and doesn't hug us.

"Where is he?" Kirk asks.

Ethan shrugs and says, "Way up on Upper Road. I wanted to show him an abandoned house, but someone was in it, so we cut across someone's property . . ."

"How far away exactly, Eth?" I demand. It's getting dark outside.

"I dunno." He blinks, looking a little surprised.

"Does he have his phone with him?" I ask.

"How should I know?" He shrugs, pushing past me on his way to the shower. Kirk reaches out and grabs Ethan by the elbow.

"Did you seriously leave him out in the woods in the dark? In the rain?" Kirk asks.

I run up the stairs to find Alex's flip phone on its charger. Then I hear the door slam downstairs.

"You are such an asshole, Ethan!" Alex screams. I run back downstairs. Alex is drenched. Snot pours from his nose, and rain runs down his sweatshirt's hood. Kirk holds him in a warm hug. Alex cries in gasps and chokes. He spits out, "You left me on the other side of the river, and I had to walk around in the dark! I saw a fucking mountain lion, you dick!"

I join Kirk in sandwiching Alex in my arms. He cries into my chest, his back heaving.

"I was so scared, Mom. I'll never trust him again!"

That night, I call Phil, the hard-ass transition mentor, and request he come over. We don't sit in on the meeting with Phil, but Ethan comes out of it saying that Phil is an asshole. Then I consult the rules set out in our contract with Ethan. He's broken the rules about unhealthy screen usage and the rules about yelling and swearing. But he's done something far more sinister: he's endangered his brother's life.

The next phone call I make is to an educational specialist to see if the therapeutic boarding schools I visited have space for Ethan. They do.

A few days later, we get a call from the dad of Ethan's friend Chester. The weekend Kirk and I had been in the cabin, Ethan had walked in the pouring rain over to Chester's house at two a.m. and knocked on a window. Apparently, while Chester slept, Ethan was thinking about a fight he'd had with him, and because he didn't have a phone or internet access, he decided to apologize in person. Only, it was the middle of the night, so rather than wait until the next day, he'd just wandered over, and Chester let him in. When Chester's dad discovered Ethan in Chester's room, Ethan explained that he was in a fugue state when he walked over and broke in. It was obviously a lie, and Chester's dad told him as much when he drove Ethan home.

Ethan had officially gone beyond just breaking the rules; he'd broken the law. Never mind that he could've been shot or arrested. We cannot help him anymore. It's obvious to Kirk, Alex, and me that all bets are off. Ethan has to go.

Before we can bust him for sneaking out, Ethan wants to talk. He says it's an emergency. We meet in his bedroom, where he tells us he hates his life. He's depressed all the time because he's making bad choices. He doesn't like himself when he lies. He is anxious. He doesn't trust his friends. He can't concentrate in school. In fact, dating back as far as kindergarten, he hasn't really learned anything in school. He can't get along with his family, and he cannot succeed in classes that are so big. Can we please put him in a school with smaller classes? Something more like his wilderness experience?

Kirk and I are relieved we don't have to tell him he's going away again. We reassure him we'll find just the right place, but he's going to have to trust us. To date, it's the most honest Ethan has been with Kirk and me. I'm heartened at how self-aware Ethan is, especially when he's dug himself into such a deep hole. I'm also glad I did the research on boarding schools before he came back from the wilderness.

We wait to hear back from the schools. In the meantime, it's President's Day weekend and time for our midwinter break. The year before, I'd taken Alex to Arizona to go horseback riding. I feel it's time to spend some one-on-one time with Eth, and I book a few days at a ranch in Wyoming where we can play on snowmobiles, go cross-country skiing, go horseback riding, and indulge in anything from skeet shooting to massages. It's my last chance to do something fun with Ethan before I have to say goodbye.

We're the only people at the resort, and we have a staff of fifty to care for us. We eat like pigs, play like wild animals, and sleep like babies. He's learned a lot from first-person shooter games and he shows me how to shoot a rifle and hit a target at the gun range. I show him how to make the perfect s'more. We play video games in the game room, and I'm content to spoil Ethan before his big sendoff.

Ethan leaves for therapeutic boarding school the last week of February. He's ready to go. We're ready for him to go. He doesn't say goodbye to his friends, but I do overhear him telling Louis, his creepy art teacher, on the phone that we're sending him away because we don't trust him, and we're assholes. Fair enough. If that's really what he feels, he'll have a lot of time to reconsider.

Kirk flies out to school with Ethan. He's struck not only by how beautiful his new school is but also that they'd celebrated his arrival at Gateway Academy with posters and streamers, like a party. Also, one of the boys from Ethan's previous wilderness adventure is one of the students. Ethan arrives at Gateway Academy because he wants to go, with a friend there to meet him. He's lucky we're able to give him a second chance in the form of a supportive residential treatment program. We're all lucky we can afford this kind of education for him. I hope Eth doesn't squander his second chance.

CHAPTER 12

Cannonball

SPRING 2019. Shortly after Ethan goes to Gateway Academy, I make good on my promise to contribute to research. I drive into San Francisco to the Mission Bay campus of UCSF. I'm at the Weill Institute for Neurosciences, participating in a study about neuroinflammation.

In the MRI scanner, the claustrophobia, nauseating and oppressive, holds me in a panic-stricken grip. I know I'm in for a long MRI, but ninety minutes is ridiculous. The radiologist at UCSF slid me into this contraption about forty-five minutes ago, but it feels like forever that I've been inside the hulking metal scanner. The radiologist has been checking on me, asking questions like, "You still okay in there?" and I lie to her when I answer in the affirmative. At least they gave me a fan so I won't be too hot.

I am pinned against the table by a helmet of sorts. The radiologist snapped it over my face and attached it to the sliding table. It keeps me from moving my head while they show me nature videos of whales eating baby seals, of decomposing dogs, and of a swarm of flying ants. This test is supposed to measure my brain activity during unpleasant images. The MRI machine makes sounds like construction workers using jackhammers.

And this isn't even as bad as a lumbar puncture.

The video stops. Through the headphones I wear, I hear the radiologist.

"Now while there's no video, we want you to look at the X on the screen. Be very still. Try to keep your eyes open," she enunciates.

I laugh a little, imagining that the radiologist is lighting a fuse and shooting me out of the MRI tube like a human cannonball. The X on the screen glares at me, as if to say, *not funny.*

I get bored of staring at the X, and my mind starts to wander a little. I feel grateful to have the bandwidth to think about my own health. Although Kirk still has some tingling in his fingers and toes, I haven't worried about my husband's health in three months.

Kirk's bounced back from chemo. He's at the office and is often around the biologists at the environmental consulting agency. They're all tree huggers, and they go fly-fishing, mountain biking, and hiking as a group. He's started competing in mountain bike races with a team from work. They train in the hills near our house. He's tried fly-fishing and loves it. He went with coworkers, and after the first time, he started taking lessons with the Casting Club in Golden Gate Park. Now, he's planning weekends away to go fly-fishing in the mountains.

In a few weeks, Kirk and I will go to visit Ethan at school. We've been getting some great letters from him, and his therapist, Matt, says he's slowly making progress. We'll be expected to participate in outdoor adventures with Eth, and I'm both excited and nervous about the prospect of rappelling down a cliff with him. We'll need to trust each other. I'll need to trust him. I start to pant, thinking about him holding the rope that keeps me from plummeting to my death.

"Do you find this stressful?" the radiologist asks. I'd forgotten I was wearing a heart rate monitor.

"No, just thinking about other stuff."

"Try to clear your mind. Just look at the screen," snaps the radiologist.

Later in the day, another researcher asks me questions that evaluate my working memory. "Lemon, airplane, yarn, mountain, cherry, butterfly," the scientist says.

I repeat the list back. She tells me a long story about a kid who goes to school and decides to pull the fire alarm. Ten minutes later, she asks me to repeat the list she gave me before. After two hours of these kinds of tests, I feel my brain is melting, but apparently I pass. Ultimately, the studies are a success, determining that I don't yet have FTD, frontotemporal dementia, which also appears in people with the C9 gene mutation.

While I'm willing to endure testing, I have my limits. They ask me to participate in another excruciating electromyography (EMG) and nerve-conduction test, just six months after my last ones. I decline. The EMG included sticking needles into my muscles to record potential chronic nerve damage. Then they ask me to surrender spinal fluid by getting a lumbar puncture. After seeing Kirk almost die from a spinal tap the previous year, I decline. Other than that, they are welcome to my working memory, my blood, my urine, my brain images. These small donations are the least I can give for such important, lifesaving research.

Before I leave, I'm encouraged to get involved in a more impactful way. I can even give my body to UCSF after I die of ALS someday. Before I have the time to process this information, the questions begin. Can they keep my genetic material in a gene bank? Can UCSF use my cadaver so students can study what ALS does to the body?

"Would you like to donate your brain to science?" a young UCSF scientist asks.

"Not while I'm still using it," I tell him. Apparently my sense of humor still works, too.

I visit Nanee in Williamsburg, Virginia. They've returned from Florida so Jimmy can check on their sports aftermarket business, which sells car flags, magnets, and tire covers to NFL aficionados. She and Jimmy have their primary residence in a gated community near a golf course. Their house, a split-level Spanish colonial with a sunken living room, is nearly impossible for Nanee to navigate, as she's not very steady on her feet with the walker and is mostly confined to a wheelchair. She can access her own bedroom and bathroom but needs to be carried or pushed down a ramp to the living room and back up again to access the kitchen, bathroom, and other bedrooms. Jimmy has thrown out his back trying to transport her. And when he goes to the office, she's alone. She's miserable, and one night, I join her in her bathroom to watch her floss her teeth. One of her hands barely works anymore, so she has to use a floss threader. She starts to cry and tells me, "I'm suffering here."

I lean over the wheelchair and hug her. I pet her hair. Seeing her like this makes my heart hurt. Tears spring to my eyes, but I don't allow them to fall down my cheeks.

"I'm so depressed," she wails. She wants to see the ocean. She feels cooped up and can't leave the house because she can't get down the front door ramp by herself. She's lost her autonomy, and the only source of joy is her mahjong group, which comes to play with her once a week.

I've learned not to urge her to get more help. But I politely ask if Jim is doing enough for her and if she has anyone else cleaning the house. Sadly, she has a paltry eight hours of help each week. Her one assistant comes to do laundry, clean the house, and buy groceries. The other helper is good at brushing and styling her hair and getting beds made. Neither one ever gets her out of the house.

"There is no way I'm going to let you sit around all day. To be happy, you need to live your life and be out in the world," I lecture.

When the laundry-and-groceries helper comes, I ask her to get Nanee dressed. Together, we push her down the front door ramp. The three of us take off down the road and roll across the golf course on the cart path. It's humid and sunny. Nanee talks about how nice it is to have the sun on her face. She hasn't been outside in weeks.

The next day, when the brushing-and-bedmaking helper comes, I insist we all go out for mani-pedis. Together, the helper and I maneuver Nanee into her car's passenger seat by using a combination of wheelchair, walker, and brute force.

Nanee all but purrs with delight when the manicurist massages her paralyzed, palsied feet. When we leave, her toes are a bright coral color, and her long fingernails have a clean white French manicure. On the way back, we stop for soft-serve ice cream. We have to eat it in the car because it's hot outside. Nanee licks the melting dessert off her finger like it's the best thing she's ever tasted.

On the last day, I talk to Jimmy. I ask him to please take Nanee back to Florida, where there's an elevator and a view of the water. They're not willing to make major renovations to their Virginia house, and it really isn't working for her. He agrees, and he helps hoist my bag into his trunk, even though his back is killing him.

When I say goodbye to Nanee, I hold back tears again. I can't picture her isolated in the house in Virginia for another minute, much less for the weeks it will take for them to move to Florida.

From the airport, I call Dadder for reassurance. He reminds

me that as people age, they don't want to give up control of their life. I need to let go and let her figure it out.

"Nanee is a strong person; she should make her own decisions," he says.

Everything he tells me makes sense, but Nanee is so stubborn. She doesn't want any strangers in her house. She doesn't want random people touching and bathing her. She wants Jimmy to do it, but Jimmy has a job and a bad back besides. She wants her independence. She doesn't want ALS. I don't want her to have ALS.

I make a silent vow to enroll in as many longitudinal studies as possible. I don't want to end up like her. I don't want Kirk, Ethan, or Alex to have to feel the frustration I feel when I'm with Nanee. I don't want my sons to have to suffer with ALS any more than I want to suffer with it.

Nanee's said that they've been looking for a cure for ALS for fifty years, and science is no closer to finding it than when they started. I know in my heart that to find a cure, I will have to submit to EMGs, spinal taps, blood draws, MRIs, speech studies, cognitive tests, nerve conduction tests, and anything that science throws my way. Amyotrophic lateral sclerosis is relentless, but so am I.

CHAPTER 13

————◆————

Untethered

SUMMER 2019. For the last two years, I've been seeing a therapist named Cynthia. When Kirk started showing early signs of cancer, I felt an anxiety that I hadn't felt before. The addition of Nanee's then-undiagnosed ALS was wearing on me, and I needed more support than I could get from my friends or family. Additionally, I was going through menopause and my sleep patterns were disrupted by night sweats. I was depleted. I felt untethered. I needed help. I needed Lexapro.

Antianxiety meds weren't the only thing that could help me with the mental hamster wheel I got onto every day. I needed the advice of a special kind of therapist: an older postmenopausal woman who knew what it meant to have a difficult child, and who knew what it was like to be a caretaker. I credit her as being the one who helps me deal with crushing anxiety over loved ones' illnesses.

Before I leave for Utah, Cynthia and I check in. She asks if I feel excited to see Ethan.

"Excited. And extremely nervous," I say.

"I'll bet. How much time do you get together?"

"A lot, but mostly in a group setting."

"Will you stay in a hotel together?" she asks. I explain that the first visit is brief. I stay in a hotel, visit Eth at school, take him out for a few hours, and then drop him back at school.

"You'll probably need the peace and quiet of a hotel after being together all day. I hope you'll make space for yourself to recharge your batteries."

I don't mention that I'd like to make space for a couple of Moscow mules each night after dropping him back at school.

My first visit with Ethan happens over Parent Weekend. I fly out to Utah and cannot believe what I see. Ethan, previously ribby and slumped over, is ten pounds heavier and standing up straighter. He's so tall that he has to nearly bend in two to hug me. He makes eye contact with me. Most importantly, he's honest. In a group therapy session, we talk about cycles of behavior. We discuss the ruts Ethan gets himself into when he's asked to do something he doesn't want to do. The session addresses his defiance toward his parents and brother. He doesn't deny it. In fact, he says, "I try to control other people, and I don't like it when I can't get people to do things my way."

It's a moment of clarity and self-awareness I didn't think he could have. I feel proud, the way I felt when Ethan first rode a bike without training wheels.

We participate in an outdoor adventure with his classmates where we rappel down a fifty-foot cliff. Ethan's an expert at climbing and rappelling because of his wilderness experience, so he has no problem getting down the cliff. I haven't rappelled since my junior high days at camp in Colorado, so I'm afraid of taking that first step backward over the edge. Matt, Eth's therapist, positions himself so he can see me and my son, previously so self-absorbed, cheer me on.

"You can do it, Mom! Just make a good base with your feet!" he yells. It takes me about fifteen minutes to get down a cliff he descends in two, but I do it, with his help. I feel closer to Ethan than I ever have. I feel like I can trust him. I feel like he cares about me.

I have a few hours each evening to spend with Ethan before he has to go back to school for bed, so we go shopping for clothes one day and then out to dinner. When he asks if we can go to a movie and I say we don't have time, he gets triggered.

He throws a temper tantrum, crying like a toddler, even though he's almost fifteen. He balls his hands into fists and stomps his foot on the pavement, right outside the restaurant. "God-fucking damn it! We never do anything *I* want to do. This is such bullshit, Mom!"

I'm disappointed some of the old behavior has come back. But I've been warned by his therapists that the kids regress around their parents on visits. The trick is to see how well they pull themselves out of the hole. He eventually stops yelling, and I'm able to return him to his dorm.

Kirk and Alex fly out the next day. As happy as they all are to see each other, Ethan and Alex don't get along as well as I hoped. Ethan refers to Alex's friends as idiots. He calls Alex "anus" when addressing him. After bullying Alex so mercilessly over the years, this is disappointing.

On a walk in Salt Lake City, Ethan refuses to stay on the same side of the street as the rest of us. He sulks when the conversation centers around anyone or anything besides himself. At the end of our last day with him, he says he misses his view of the mountains. He wants to go back to school. We want him to go back too.

Once home, I hear back from one of the agents I've queried. Her name is Sandra. She's read the first fifty pages of *Unnatural Resources* but has been busy moving from California to Alabama and finally answers me.

She wants to sign me as a client but doesn't know if we'll work well together. Do I want to come to stay with her for a few days and have her review my book? My writing partners, Shannon and Dorothy, disapprove of Sandra. They think she's going to take advantage of me. Sandra says there are so many writers who won't take her advice that she no longer trusts them to listen to her. When I ask my therapist, Cynthia, for advice, she says, "Is it a financial hardship for you to go?"

"No," I say. She asks if I have anything better to do,

anything more life-affirming to do than to hear a couple of days' worth of praise for my book.

"Of course not," I tell her. She says I should go. So I do.

I spend four days in Huntsville. Not exactly the kind of place my left-leaning soul cares to frequent, but duty calls. Sandra hosts me in her gigantic Southern plantation house, where she and her husband feed me like I am royalty. I have an enormous bedroom and bathroom to myself, plus a kitchen and living area where we spend three long days deconstructing my book. As much praise as she has for the writing, she wants me to change a lot. In fact, some of her suggestions are unacceptable. She wants me to cut a third of the narrative and replace it with a different character's story. Do I really want to work with someone who wants to see such a different version of *Unnatural Resources*?

She invites one of her other writers over for dinner. He's about my age and very flirty. It's clear that not only are they great friends, but there's something about the dinner that seems a bit like a chaperoned first date. Like she maybe wants to fix us up. He's recently divorced and looks at me like he's interested in something more than just convincing me to collaborate with his agent.

Sandra and her husband take me out for dinner one night. We eat a traditional Southern meal: a meat and three. That's meat, plus three sides, like potato salad, greens, corn fritters, corn muffins, black-eyed peas. Over dinner, she reassures me she wants to represent me. Sandra definitely feeds me well, but this trip is a moneymaking venture for her to deconstruct my book. It has a $4,900 price tag. I am under the impression that after I commit to flying across the country to spend time with her, she will offer to represent me.

Before I leave, I ask her if she will be my agent. She tells me I should expect a contract within a few weeks. It's a lie.

I check in with Sandra once a month for three months. Every time, she tells me she's up to her ears in work, but the contract is on its way. It isn't.

"What did you learn from that experience?" asks Cynthia, my therapist.

"I learned not to trust agents," I tell her.

We get a panicky phone call from the owner of Gateway. Ethan has been "recruiting" kids on his floor to gang up on the newer boys.

"We don't allow kingpins here, and if he can't change this behavior, we'll ask him to leave," the head of the school warns us. Kirk and I take this seriously. If the therapeutic boarding school can't live with him, we have no chance.

As a punishment, they'll instate an arms-length protocol. Eth will need to be within two feet of a staff member at all times. That means someone will be standing outside the shower when he's in the bathroom. It also means he cannot return to the room he shares with three other boys. He will have to sleep out in the hall on a mattress. Additionally, he will not be allowed to speak to or eat with any boy until his behavior becomes more acceptable.

Within a week, Ethan's behavior seems to turn. He does his level best to be respectful to others. He admits to trying to manipulate and control the other boys at school. He starts being much more honest, even on the phone with Alex, who he admits does not deserve to be treated badly. He also says the only reason he was disrespectful to Alex was that he was jealous of his little brother: Jealous that Alex likes school. Jealous that Alex has a girlfriend and a large group of friends he could play music with. Most importantly, he admits that he feels inferior to his brother. He thinks there is something wrong with him. And he knows in his heart the problem is the way he treats others.

His floormates notice a difference in Ethan. He seems more open, more vulnerable to them. And when he asks to be a leader on his floor, they start to trust him. Ethan is so well-behaved that he is granted a visit to see Nanee. After another Parent Weekend, when Ethan teaches me how to scale an eighty-foot cliff, we go to the airport together and fly to Florida, where we meet up with Kirk and Alex. On the plane, Ethan tells me, "This weekend isn't about me; it's about Nanee."

We stay at our usual place, the rental across the street from Nanee's condo. I'm struck with how demonstrative Ethan is with Kirk, Alex, and me. He can't get enough hugging. He also makes an enormous effort to help Nanee. He pushes her wheelchair when we take her out to dinner. He makes her lunch and clears the plates. Finally, he's participating in life like the rest of us. He contributes like someone who cares about others. He has empathy.

I'm delighted to see Ethan and Alex sitting out on Nanee's balcony, talking one day. They aren't fighting or competing with each other. I turn my back for a minute, and suddenly I hear sobbing from the balcony. I poke my head outside.

"Everything okay?" I ask. Turning his head and facing me, Ethan wipes tears from his eyes. To my surprise, he's smiling.

"Mom, leave us alone," Alex gulps. He's laughing so hard, he's crying too.

I shrug and leave them to their fun, happy that they're enjoying each other's company. Nanee needs my help in the kitchen. She's making matzoh ball soup.

This feels so familiar. I take my mother's hands in mine, try to uncurl them under the faucet. Her left hand is clawed, now permanently stuck, rigored. I don't exactly know how to wash an adult's hands, but it's kind of like washing my kids' hands when they were toddlers. But not quite. She has a large sapphire ring on her left ring finger. Her nails are at least an inch long, and then, there's the claw. That's different.

"Wait a sec, Nan," I say. I run my own hands under the faucet and soap them up. I use way more suds than I need to. I reach for her left hand and massage the soap between her fingers. I use my thumbnail to pick the matzoh meal from under her fingernails. I rinse and take her other hand in mine. It occurs to me that were I not here, she'd have to deal with the matzoh balls herself, cracking eggs, pouring oil, opening the box of matzoh meal, rolling it into ping-pong balls, one-handed. I look away from her hands to her face. She smiles ruefully at me and shrugs, like she knows. There are so many firsts on this trip. The first time I'm taller than her because she can't stand anymore. The first time she talked about what she wants to be buried in. The first time I washed her hands.

I grab the gooseneck faucet and rinse her hands. She doesn't thank me; she's on a mission. She's not going to cry.

"Okay. Time to check the broth. Is it boiling yet?" she slurs. She halfway dries her hands on the paper towel I give to her. Nanee puts the wheelchair into reverse and aims for the stove, which she cannot reach. On her way, she rolls over a little blob of dough she's dropped. The electric wheelchair flattens it, leaving a slug-shaped smear on the floor. I bend over and wipe it up with the paper towel she's also dropped. Everything is a colossal effort for her now. A simple act like washing hands, using the bathroom, or picking up something off the floor is nearly impossible.

Before she can reach for the pot on the stove, I say, "I've got it."

The soup's not boiling yet anyway. As I stare into the pot of chicken broth, it strikes me that this is maybe the last meal she'll make with me. It's important for me to make memories with Nanee. There's so little time left.

"Not yet," I tell her, but I don't know if I'm talking about the soup or something more dire.

"Okay, then let's clean this up," she mumbles. She points with her good hand at the empty boxes, the eggshells, and the oil bottle. She watches me throw the boxes into the recycling, grab the eggshells, and throw them in the trash. As I reach for the oil, Jimmy bursts through the front door.

"Hey, girls. It smells great in here! Is it cocktail time yet? Mindy, you want something?"

Nanee says something I can't quite make out. She must be ready for a rest in front of CNN. I check the soup again, which is boiling vigorously. I turn down the heat and reach for the matzoh balls.

"I'm good," I tell Jimmy, who pours Nanee a plastic cup of ice water. He kisses me on the head on his way to her. I hear my boys bang the door shut on their way back across the street. Carefully, I lower each dough ball into the roiling pot of broth.

"Excuse me," Nanee says, motoring off in the direction of the master bathroom. Jim follows her in, calling over his shoulder, "Duty calls."

As the pot fills with matzoh balls, I realize that the intimacy we share only goes so far. She won't let me take her to the bathroom, shower with her, or tuck her in bed at night. She won't let me put her bra on or help her with her makeup.

Sharing the moment, washing her hands, and rolling matzoh balls was enough for her. I rinse the sticky plate where the matzoh balls left their round footprints and put it in the dishwasher.

I let myself out into the hallway and take the elevator down to the street. My shirt smells strongly of chicken broth, so I walk into the humid Florida air and head across the street to our vacation rental to change for dinner.

There's a mother duck in the storm gutter on the side of the road. She and her eleven ducklings seem unperturbed when I walk by them. Dragonflies are everywhere in the autumn afternoon along the Gulf Coast. They whiz by me, so close that I can hear the hum of their wings. I wonder if I'll be in a wheelchair one day and if someone will take care of me when I can't take care of myself. For now, I'm grateful to walk on the sprinkler-soaked pavement, to unlock and open the rusty gate, and to climb the stairs to our rental condo.

As I enter the small unit, Kirk and the boys each greet me with a hug. My kids are both taller than I am, but I can stand and hug them and bury my face in their shoulders and cry the tears of gratitude, of sadness, of love that only I can cry.

CHAPTER 14

Being There

AUTUMN 2019. I'm not the only person attending to the needs of older generations. Kirk, whose parents are both deceased, learns about his stepmother's need to move into assisted living. Her own kids have moved her into a memory care facility, as she's unable to live on her own. Anita's been living in the house where Kirk grew up since Kirk's father died. Because his dad passed the house down to him, Kirk is tasked with flying out to Colorado, cleaning it out, and getting it ready to go on the market. The job seems insurmountable. Anita's own kids, in their haste to move her into assisted living, have left the house looking like a tornado has struck.

Kirk takes an entire week off just to empty the place. He works eighteen-hour days, calling Goodwill, filling a giant dumpster, and driving back and forth to the local dump. The house is so dirty he refuses to sleep on any of the beds. He opts for an inflatable air mattress and a sleeping bag. Within two days, he's stressed himself sick. By the end of the week, there is still work to be done. The house needs new kitchen appliances, new carpet, and new paint. And the broken hot tub in the backyard has to be removed.

We hardly talk that week, but when we do, I tell him I'm concerned about his emotional well-being because he's isolated in a depressing physical space and doesn't spend much time with his friends or family. I'm concerned about his physical well-being because it's only been a year since chemo ended, and he frequently feels unwell. When he comes home, he looks awful. His eyes are red, and he looks like he's aged ten years in one week. He goes straight to bed and sleeps for five hours. I cook him dinner, and he goes back to sleep, this time for twelve.

The next morning, I'm sipping coffee and reading a magazine when he comes downstairs, puts a CD in the stereo, and turns it up loud. I'm instantly irritated, given that I've spent the week he was gone holding down the fort, hosting Alex's garage band practices, driving him to appointments, and spending my writing time entertaining the masses during half days of school. It's my first Saturday morning to have some much-needed quiet time. As glad as I am that he's home, I'm very unhappy with him. I tell him as much: although he's been alone for a week, now he's home, and he has to learn to live with the rest of us. It quickly becomes an argument, not about stereos and coffee but about the nature of our relationship.

It's an all-day fight where nobody pulls any punches. He's pissed that I don't appreciate that he had to take off work to go clean up someone else's mess. I'm mad that he doesn't make the effort to understand what was going on in my world when he was gone. He accuses me of not having a job because I'm just an unpaid writer. I accuse him of devaluing my work. He accuses me of criticizing him when he's sick—of kicking him when he's down. And so on.

At the center for me is that he doesn't consider my writing to be work. Since age seventeen, I've been a serious writer. I wrote music for eight years in a band called 40th Day. I wrote, produced, and sold a feature film. It took me twelve years. I worked on my Congo book for eight, have contributed to two anthologies. He replies, "Well, I don't think your writing hobby is work because you don't get paid."

I'm stung. The lack of a paycheck has no bearing on whether what one does is work. What if I get published? Then is it work? Does Stephen King have a better job than mine because he is making money at it? What if his books were never published? Would it still be his life's work?

But I also take issue with his devaluing my job as a stay-home parent. It is arguably the most important unpaid job there is. And caretaking a kid like Ethan is a formidable task. For at least fifteen years, I've had to engage with him every time I told him "no" or had to enforce a rule. He has been moody, disrespectful, and dishonest. I have been the one to goad him into the car to go to a therapist, tutor, or specialist. I've been the one to research the meds, treatments, and schools. I'm also the one who sees him off to school and have been the whipping boy between after-school activities and dinnertime. And caretaking Kirk, who is an unpleasant sick person, when he had cancer (twice) is no less formidable than parenting Ethan. I often feel underappreciated for the work I do. I don't get snaps for saving Kirk's life after his lumbar puncture. Nobody cheers me on when I finish the end of a draft of my novel. I rarely get thanks of acknowledgment for being the only parent who ever tried to improve Ethan's life by sending him to a better school. My activism in Congo isn't recognized.

I suspect that deep down, Kirk is unhappy or jealous because I come from the kind of inherited wealth that doesn't require that I work for others. I can afford to work without a paycheck, while he cannot. It's not an easily remedied difference between us because we keep our finances separate. Before we were married in 2001, my family pressured us to enter a prenuptial agreement. Neither Kirk nor I wanted to do so, but in California, anything acquired by either person in a couple becomes joint property. In the case of divorce, everything is split between former spouses. My dad left my mom when I was little. I'd already seen how a long, acrimonious divorce could wear down a family. Maybe deep down, I was concerned that our relationship was destined to fail.

We hash it out a few days later.

"If you can't handle that I don't get paid to write this book, I am happy to go out and get a job waiting tables," I tell him.

"That's stupid. You're worth, like, a gazillion dollars," he says.

"I would much rather burn the fucking prenup and not have this kind of fight with you ever again," I say.

"We only entered that agreement because you don't trust men not to leave," Kirk says.

"I trust you not to leave. Sometimes I just don't trust you not to die," I say.

"Sometimes I don't trust myself not to die either," he says. "I didn't mean what I said. I know how hard you're working on this book. I think I was just sick and tired of being sick and tired."

It's an uneasy truce because we'll never be on equal financial footing.

The fight makes me reevaluate the way I perceive myself. Being the primary caregiver is a thankless job, so the accolades have to come from within. Nobody will acknowledge my work trying to end genetically inherited ALS. This is another part of letting go, surrendering the expectation that anyone will care.

I know who I am: universal mother, musician, friend, activist, writer, donor, filmmaker, sister, daughter. I have learned how to surrender all other things, but I will have to fight for who I am and what I believe in. This will make it easier for me to face the monster under my bed.

My next appointment at UCSF will review how my ALS has progressed, if at all. I look forward to my drive down to the Mission Bay campus, where, no doubt, I will have to submit to another EMG and MRI. I actually relish the idea of a spinal tap now, especially if it advances ALS research. My life's work as a caretaker now includes Nanee, my kids, and my future grandkids. Finding the cure for ALS will be the ultimate sacrifice and gift to my family.

As far as I'm concerned, nobody besides me has to give me snaps now. As far as I'm concerned, the monster under my bed doesn't stand a chance.

The week before Thanksgiving, I receive emails from Ethan's school. The subjects are titled "Your Son's First Visits Home" and "Transitions." I know it means that Ethan has progressed far enough in his ten months at therapeutic boarding school that he'll earn a few days at home soon. We're about to pick him up to visit Nanee for Thanksgiving. It's already a miracle she's lived a year past her neurologist's prediction. It's a bigger miracle Ethan will be coming home soon. And with every miracle, there's bound to be a flip side. With Nanee's living longer, she'll be encountering more challenges: eating, fending for herself in the bathroom, getting out of the house, and communicating. With Ethan's coming home, there will also be challenges: his impulse control, his desire to see pot-smoking and law-breaking friends, his bullying of Alex.

As we pack to go to Nanee's, we speculate about Ethan's visit. The school allows the kids two weeks to go on vacation, but how many days can we reasonably handle? How many of those days will Kirk be able to take off work? Will Eth be able to access the internet at home? A cell phone? A digital camera? His alcohol-based markers? Will we need to start hiding the devices and our wallets again? How will Ethan get along with the rest of us? Is it even safe?

I have true reservations about his return. He still hasn't been able to sustain more than a few hours of respectful behavior toward his little brother. Per the school's rules, we still can't let him out of our sight, unless he's in the bathroom. I've gotten used to a peaceful house, one where I can leave my thirteen-year-old Alex alone for hours. One where I can shower with the bathroom door unlocked. One where I don't have to worry about someone sneaking out or breaking the law.

When I truly explore my feelings, I don't really want Ethan to come home yet. Kirk calls me on it, more than once. He asks why I'm so nervous to be left alone with Ethan. After sixteen years of parenting him, I'm surprised he even asks. Is it possible Kirk still believes it was wrong to send him to boarding school? Does he not see our child has cognitive disabilities compounded by a severe lack of self-control? Does he not recognize being a stay-home working parent of Ethan is the single most stressful thing I have ever done?

I ask Matt, Ethan's therapist, how many days we can "look forward to" when Ethan comes home. Matt wants to address it in family therapy, over Skype.

"Mindy, do you want to tell Ethan how you feel about his coming home for a visit?" he asks directly. I can't tell a lie. Eth's been asked to confront his truth, and now it's time for me to confront mine.

"I have my trepidations, and I'm nervous we're not ready," I say.

"What are you nervous about?" Matt asks.

"I'm afraid I won't be able to hold boundaries with you and you'll revert to some of the less trustworthy behaviors that you used to have."

"I'm nervous too, Mom," Ethan says, surprising me. He won't make eye contact over Skype; he stares at the floor in front of him. "I don't want to have power struggles with you and Dad. I don't want to bully my brother."

It's a turning point for us. All along, I've thought he liked being the enemy. I thought he found it powerful. The conversation progresses. He admits again the reason he bullies Alex is that he's jealous of him.

"Things come easily to Alex. He likes school. He has a girlfriend. He has a bunch of friends—"

Matt interrupts him, "Now turn it around, Eth. What is it you think is wrong with you?"

Ethan says there must be something wrong with him because he's the one in a residential treatment facility. He doesn't have any friends. He doesn't do well in school. Matt continues to push him.

"Why are you here, Eth?" he asks.

"Because I try to control people. And they don't like that," Ethan answers correctly.

Matt says, "And tell me who you hung out with yesterday."

"My friends at school," Eth explains.

"Your friends?" he asks. "And do you control them?"

"No, because I've learned how not to," Ethan says. He grins at the screen.

"In school? The same place you have a 3.8 GPA?"

At this point, we're all giggling. I ask Ethan, "If you have friends, if you're getting A's and B's in school, and if you're about to come home, why are you jealous of Alex?"

"I don't know."

He notes that sometimes he feels he has nothing in common with Alex. Alex is an actor and a musician. Ethan likes rock climbing and graffiti art. I can't help but think about the differences between myself and my brother, who is also two and a half years younger. I am a writer and a musician. He's a teacher and an athlete. He listens to System of a Down. I like Radiohead. He watches sports. I watch *The Walking Dead*.

I've never perceived the arrival of my little brother as a detriment to my life. Our friendship has been forged over the years, but we've always loved each other. I think Ethan's never recovered from the birth of his brother, and he's still looking for reasons to hate him. And the part that really kills me is sometimes, when you least expect it, you need your sibling.

When my parents' relationship started to tank, Brian and I clung to each other. We were a source of comfort for one another. Without my job of helping to raise my little brother, I probably wouldn't have felt such a sense of purpose in my junior high and high school years. And he certainly wouldn't have weathered the storm very well either.

I remember the day Nanee told me and Brian to take Dadder's clock radio out onto the driveway. The cicadas were humming. It must've been summer. Nanee brought out two hammers from the toolbox in the garage. Her nails were always an inch or more long, and it was strange seeing her manicured fingers around such crude instruments.

"Let's have a smashing party!" she suggested. Brian, who always ran hot, was already sweating. Droplets ran from under his curls onto his neck and down his back.

"What do you mean? That's Daddy's," he said. He knew better than to break other people's things. Nanee set the radio on the pavement. I can only imagine what the neighbors were thinking. The honors Spanish teacher was standing at the end of her driveway, kneeling over a radio with her hammer-holding hand aloft. Had she lost her mind?

"Come on! It's fun! Smash it!" she cried, bringing the hammer down. The radio was solid state and strong, so she put down the hammer, picked up the radio, and winged it to the ground. It cracked in two. Little springs and tubes rolled onto the street. I sat down on one of the white boulders at the end of our driveway. My terry cloth running shorts were pretty skimpy, and the back of my thigh stuck to the rock. Brian sat on the boulder across from me, wiping sweat from his brow. We stared at our mother.

Later, after everyone went to bed, I pushed aside my drapes and stared out the window onto the driveway. I knew that I'd never hear my dad's car come into the garage again. As I looked out on the remnants of my dad's smashed radio, there was a knock on my door. Brian came in with tear-stained cheeks.

"Can't you sleep?" I asked him. He shook his head and pulled at his curls.

"Want me to sleep in your other bed?" I asked. He nodded. That was the first of many nights I spent in his room. When I remember that night, I think of my sons.

When Kirk was diagnosed with cancer, Ethan never reached out to Alex, who is just about the most trustworthy and loyal person I know. Because of Ethan's hostility toward his little brother, he'd deprived himself, and Alex, of what they needed most: each other.

What if Kirk got sick again? What if I got sick? Would Ethan be there for his little brother? Would Alex be there for Eth?

CHAPTER 15

Thanksgiving

AUTUMN 2019. Unbelievably, we are all assembled again. Nanee, more than a year past her expected survival date, is hosting Thanksgiving. She's completely confined to a wheelchair, but her nails are still manicured, and her makeup is perfect. She orders Jimmy around, the way she always has, making him pick up ice bags from the 7-Eleven, set the tables, and drive around to buy extra beach chairs at the local surf shop.

Alex and I fly in and immediately notice the changes in the condo. The master bathroom door is off the hinges, for easier wheelchair access. Erin, Nanee's new helper, spends several hours at the condo, doing laundry, curling Nanee's hair, and mixing protein shakes that Nanee reluctantly drinks.

When Alex and Jimmy are out buying beach chairs and fishing nets, Erin, Nanee, and I are all working in the kitchen. Erin twists Nanee's hair around a curling iron. Wearing nurses' scrubs, Erin has a conspicuous Boston accent. She brags, "Before I went to nursing school, I was a hairdresser."

"Isn't she great?" Nanee slurs. It's getting harder for her to talk these days, and harder for us to understand her, too. I pour a bottle of chocolate protein drink into the blender. In the four hours since Erin arrived, she's arranged a cornucopia of fruit and flowers, done two loads of laundry, made Nanee's lunch, prepped all the Thanksgiving veggies, made the gravy base, loaded the dishwasher, and taken Nanee to the bathroom twice. She's more than capable, but it's the other things I really appreciate. Erin hugs my mom, and on more than one occasion I hear her tell Nanee, "I love you."

When Erin leaves, Nanee tells her to enjoy her family. Erin hugs Nanee goodbye and then turns to me.

"Thanks so much for taking such great care of my mom," I tell Erin, hugging her. When we're alone, Nanee motors over to the balcony. I'm amazed she can still operate the chair. One hand works just enough, and her claw can still hold the glass with the shake in it.

"Watch out. I'm drinking and driving," she jokes. We position ourselves in the sun, overlooking the Gulf. I can hear children playing in the surf below us and can sense Nanee's jealousy of all the things others can do but she can't. I feel impotent compared to Erin and want to do more for her.

"I know you like it when I come, but it's not helpful if I just sit here and chat with you," I tell her. "I want to be of service."

She looks at me as if wondering if I'm up to the task. I stare back at her. She puts the shake on the coffee table.

"Okay, then. You want to be of real service? Follow me."

She turns the chair toward her bedroom. She has me sit at the foot of her bed, take her slippers off, and put her AFOs on. It's not easy. She doesn't have any muscles left in her foot, so I'm basically handling dead meat, like a fish or a really big chicken breast. It flops around until I get the brace on.

Then she has me hand her a heavy cloth belt, which she struggles to get around her waist and fasten in front. She's shaking, but I don't know why until she motors in the direction of the bathroom. Instinctively, I bring her walker, knowing she can't transfer directly from the chair to the toilet. She parks outside the bathroom and tells me to position the walker in front of her. She wants me to pull her up from behind by the belt. I grab it, feeling her bony back and ribs under my knuckles.

"Doesn't this hurt?" I ask, afraid of bruising her.

"Nope. Just go!" she gasps, grabbing the walker. With what seems like a colossal effort and the last bit of her strength, she pulls herself to a standing position at the walker. I've gotten used to seeing her seated and dumbly remember that once upon a time, she was a lot taller than me. She takes one step toward the toilet and says, "Okay, pull my pants down."

I do and realize that she's not wearing underwear. This is the intimacy I've been missing. The trust I don't feel she has in me. Suddenly, I feel very grown-up. Nanee is standing half naked in front of me. She turns while clutching the grab bar and sits (or falls) onto the raised toilet. I take a step back toward the door. I don't want to invade her privacy while she pees.

"Don't go. I still need you," she says.

I feel grateful and relieved she can still wipe herself. While Nanee sits on the toilet, she uses a baby wipe to wash her hands. It's just too hard for her to use the sink. She pulls herself back up to a standing position, holding onto the walker for dear life. I pull her pants up, noting that her hips are so skinny she'll need a pair with a smaller waist soon.

What will happen when she can't get onto the toilet? What if she can't wipe? Who will change her diapers? Jimmy? Erin? Me? I push the thoughts out of my head, knowing that this moment, here with Nanee, is a turning point for us.

She maneuvers herself over the wheelchair. I grab her by the belt from behind and lower her into the chair. After she takes off the belt, we sit by the balcony again. She's still shaking, even though she's just peed. Then I realize she's been holding back tears. They come in a torrent. I stand and hug her head to my chest. I pet her hair and tell her, "It's okay, Nanee. You can trust me."

"It's not about trust. It's just that you're the kid and I'm the parent!" she sobs. All this time I thought she didn't think I was worthy of her trust. I had the feeling she didn't think I was capable of caring for her. That she was too proud to accept help from me.

"Thank you for letting me help you. I feel honored that you let me in," I tell her. I grab a Kleenex and give it to her. She wipes her eyes and holds onto the tissue, like she might need it again later. I feel a confidence I didn't have before, and I high-five her. She laughs, even with the tears streaming down her face.

Brian and his family arrive in the evening, the day before Thanksgiving. His kids have changed so much since the last time I saw them. Brendan, now a college freshman, walks with the confidence of a man and drinks wine with us at dinner. Kevin is six foot four, and at sixteen, still growing. He tells us about the infection he has in his arm and updates Brian every fifteen minutes on various sports stats. Olivia is ten. She's tall and thin to begin with, but her weight has dropped significantly since the last time I saw her. Her competitive dance clubs have her very busy.

For Brian and Elaine's kids, it's a lot to take in: Nanee's declining health and growing needs have them anxious. Ethan and Kirk haven't even arrived from Utah yet. Who knows if Eth will be able to rise to the occasion and go with the flow? Thanksgiving will be lots of people in Nanee and Jimmy's small condo. It's a lot of moving parts. We've all been asked to provide something. Their friends, Rich and Joey, will bring mashed potatoes, cranberries, and dessert. Brian will make the stuffing and baste the turkey. I will make sweet potatoes with Ethan. Olivia will make the cheese and crudité platter. Kirk and Jimmy will be in the kitchen to carve the turkey.

When Kirk and Eth arrive, it feels like we've all come home. Ethan nearly folds himself in two to hug me, and I marvel at the size of him. He's getting to look more like Kirk every day. Ethan is excited. It looks as if he's on track to come home for a visit soon.

Kirk, newly healed from his trip to Grand Junction, is his old self again. The look on his face mirrors my own feelings—like we all belong together, like their joining us completes the puzzle.

Thanksgiving comes off like a Broadway production that was just in Tech Week. Nanee spends her day orchestrating everything. She has Brian over to put the turkey in early in the morning. No doubt this is to get him alone in the kitchen, away from the excitement of five grandkids in her space. Kirk crosses the street to work on chopping veggies for a crudité plate. I bring our kids over a little later, and Alex makes a beeline for the beach. Ethan visits with Jimmy.

Several times, I check in on the action in Nanee's kitchen. Nanee looks really tired. Her head lists a little to one side, and she frequently wipes her mouth with a tissue. One of the final symptoms of her ALS is the changes to bulbar function, like drooling and choking. Sometimes, when I see her like that, drooling and dabbing, I find myself hoping that she'll die peacefully in her sleep soon. I feel guilty, wanting her to die, but she's in such sorry shape. She's lost her independence, and her dignity will be the next thing to go. I can't imagine Nanee will be able to stand drooling and choking in front of people. It's beyond me that she'll ever allow anyone but Jim, Erin, or me to take her to the bathroom.

She recruits me to baste the turkey, and Brian and I wrestle the giant bird out of the oven so I can reach it without burning myself. We all sit at her table and chat about the grandkids. There is no conversation about what her next fight against ALS will be. We don't talk about her will, her Do Not Resuscitate order, or what she's going to wear in the coffin. The Bears game is on, and both she and Brian have bigger fish to fry.

They make their way to the big-screen television, and in a second, the game is blaring from the living room. The constant cleanup during Thanksgiving prep has me loading the dishwasher, soaping up pots, and running the garbage disposal. I eventually run out of things to do, so I take an hour to myself. Between Jimmy and everyone else, Nanee is not going to hurt herself.

I've spent two days by Nanee's side, and getting out into the fresh air feels liberating. I wonder how often Jimmy takes an hour to himself. Does he run out to the grocery store or golf when she's alone? The heat from the pavement radiates through the bottoms of my shoes. I pass so many senior citizens, I lose count. They're all old, and they're all walking on the sidewalk. Some even have canes and are older than Nanee by a lot. I feel so sorry for her. I marvel at my own body. The moving toes connected to the flexing foot. The hand that clutches the water bottle. I am grateful I can walk, and have learned not to take anything for granted, especially my health.

When I return, I ask Ethan if he wants to make the sweet potatoes with me. Nanee's kitchen is too crowded with kids and grandkids, so we'll be working on them at our condo. On our way out of Nanee's building, we run into Elaine, who is piling her kids into their rental van. Without thinking, I ask, "Anyone want to come over to make sweet potatoes with us?"

Olivia and Brendan join us, and we cross the street together, chatting about how much homework Brendan has in college. We file into our kitchen, and I assume the same role as Nanee, delegating jobs to everyone. With help from Ethan, Olivia will open the cans, Brendan will drain the yams and dump them into the pot. Ethan will find the casserole dish, and Olivia will cut the butter. Brendan will heat the pot. Ethan's in charge of the marshmallows. I'm not sure about this dynamic. Ethan has been put into the middle-child position and won't be able to control anyone.

I'd promised Eth we'd do this together, and I don't want him to get mad at me. It's a difficult trip, and the last thing we need is an altercation in front of the cousins. I close my eyes and take a deep breath.

While Brendan dumps the first can of sweet potatoes into the pot, I see Ethan put his hand on Livvy's shoulder. It's enormous on her tiny frame. She looks up at him.

"Need some help?" he asks her. She nods. He takes the can opener from her and says, "You squeeze it until you hear it pop. See?"

He hands it back to her and she tries it herself. I hear the pop from across the room. He pats her reassuringly on the back and says, "Good job! You did it!"

It's a gesture I've seen so many times from Alex around other kids. This sweetness and compassion. Empathy and protectiveness. It's love, plain and simple.

I realize in this moment Ethan has faced the monster under his bed and is beating it. We all have monsters under our beds, whether they're anger management, cancer, anxiety, or ALS. We all have the option to throw a bigger comforter over the bed and hope the monster will go away. The problem is that if we don't face off against these beasts, they tend to grow and get more deadly.

If we battle our monsters, we can eventually win. Eth is living proof of this.

CHAPTER 16

Legendary Crier

WINTER 2019. I visit Nanee again between Christmas and New Year's. I've been getting text updates from Jimmy. She's confined to her bed. She eats only soft foods, like Jell-O, ice cream, and soups. She wears Depends undergarments and never uses the toilet. She still insists on having as little help as possible, but she finally concedes to allow hospice to take over her medical care. Every few days, someone comes by to give her a sponge bath, check her meds (which are mostly painkillers and strong antidepressants). She's been on morphine for a few days, and her speech is very garbled.

When I arrive, the door to her bedroom is closed and Jimmy meets me at the door. He's limping, his hair is matted, and it smells like he hasn't showered in days. The condo is a mess, too. Wilted flowers slouch in dirty vases and foul the air with their murky water.

"How you doing, Peep?" he asks, and before I can tell him, he says, "She's finally asleep. Don't wake her up."

I look past him at the kitchen table, which is piled with unsigned checks for his employees. It's Christmas bonus time, and he's trying to beat the clock by getting the mail out. Only he's so busy caring for Nanee, he never has time to sign checks, shower, clean the house, or go out with friends. He's in the trenches, the way the parent of a newborn is. No time for anything, especially sleep. When I hug him, he wilts, like a dead flower. It feels like he might faint in my arms.

"I think you should go take a nap. I can be here when she wakes up," I offer. He shakes his head and tells me there's no way. Nanee will only allow him to care for her. I offer to go to the grocery store, and he tells me, "You don't know what she needs. Plus, I gotta get outta here, stretch my legs."

None of it makes sense. They have the money to hire a private duty nurse. They can get eight hours during the day and ten hours at night. They even have an extra bedroom, where Jim can sleep if Nanee's awake at night.

When the hospice social worker, Carly, comes by, I corner her before she can check on Nanee. I ask her how to get them more help, and she explains that she's not qualified to recommend other nurses.

"What if this were your dad, trying to care for your mom?" I ask, pointing to Jim, who has fallen asleep with his head on the table.

"Then I'd hire JT Private Duty. They're the best in the area," she whispers. I suggest, when Nanee wakes up, we all meet with her and Jim together and insist that they get more help. As if on cue, we hear Nanee's voice over the baby monitor in the kitchen. Jimmy bolts upright, and we follow him into the bedroom. I can barely hold my tears in when I see her. She wears no makeup and has tubes in her nose. Because she has trouble breathing, she's propped up on several pillows in a hospital bed. She is doped up and she can't find her glasses, which are right next to her, stuck into a pocket of her bed.

She recognizes me, thank God, and pats the bed next to her, mumbling, "Hi, Peep."

I sit next to her and hold her hand. Everything seems to melt away. I'm not thinking about Ethan, about cancer, or about my own risk of developing ALS. I only have compassion for her. And even though she can't say it, I know she's glad I'm here. Within a few minutes, she's asleep again. Eventually, Jim wakes her up again to give her more drugs. I broach the subject of more care in the house. With Jimmy and Carly there, she can't really say no. Her Depends brief is wet, and Jim throws Carly and me out so he can change her. Because he's so gimpy with a bad back, a sore toe, and cataracts, the task takes a lot longer than it would for someone like me. I take the opportunity to call JT Private Duty. Within fifteen minutes, I've lined up sixteen hours of care each day.

My phone never stops pinging. Between JT Private Duty, hospice, Brian, Kirk, and Dadder texting, I can barely spend the time I need to with Nanee. I put my phone away once I've gotten a nurse to come over to interview with us. Before

Carly leaves, I get her phone number. She seems to be the only one who can think clearly about Nanee's needs.

Jim's sisters, Carol and Peggy, are in town for the Christmas holiday. I put together an appetizer plate, start a load of laundry, throw away some old flowers, and straighten up the kitchen. As I ready the house, Erin, their part-time helper, comes back. She loves Nanee, and she respects me enough to be honest with me.

"I'd be surprised if she lives another month. It's good you're here, but you should have Brian and your Aunt Melissa come too."

I appreciate her honesty, but I need more information. I ask her when the last time was that Nanee moved her bowels. I ask when she last ate a solid meal. When she last left the apartment. Erin shrugs and says, "She doesn't do that stuff anymore, but Jimmy's sisters are coming, so I'm here to do her makeup and hair."

Erin is the lifeline for Nanee's dignity. She brings her soft pajamas, makes her smoothies, and lets her rail against Trump when Jimmy is out at the grocery store. She's grateful that I hired JT and makes no attempt to hide her relief.

Nanee is awake again. She asks me, "How much does JT cost?"

I shake my head and say, "Don't worry about that. Brian and I can manage it."

"I'm not letting you pay for it!" she murmurs. I'm glad Erin is doing her hair. Nanee would be way more upset if she weren't being preened. I stand over her and try not to cross my arms over my chest or put my fists on my hips. I shake my head in dismay and say, "Erin can only work so many hours, and you won't let me move in. Jim's a wreck. He needs a break. He needs to sleep."

I don't want her to feel guilty, but she fights back, saying, "He just wants to go out and drink beers with the guys while I lie here dying!"

I can tell I'm being played and say, "He's giving you all he can give and more. He's got a bad back, and he doesn't get any sleep—"

"But he has plenty of energy to go out and take a walk and get a beer!" she snaps.

I can't fight like this. It's unwinnable. She's dying of one of the most miserable diseases known, and she wants the man in her life to take care of her all the time. She doesn't want a nurse, or me, or Brian. She doesn't want assisted living. But what she wants is becoming impossible.

"Please promise me you'll just make the effort to meet this nurse from JT. If you don't like her, I promise, I will not fly back to California until we find someone you like. Deal?"

"Okay. Now let's go through my jewelry. I want you to know where it all goes when I'm gone." And like that, the conversation is over. Erin has made Nanee look like a million bucks, and by the time Jim's sisters arrive, we've gone through all the jewelry.

That night, Nanee is in good form. She actually gets out of bed with the help of the JT Private nurse, a stout red-haired woman named Micky. Micky gets Nanee to eat a real meal: a pulled barbecued pork sandwich, coleslaw, and a Coke. Nanee has trouble with the electric wheelchair and keeps rolling over her oxygen cords, but she's able to eat with Jimmy and his sisters at the table. I go back to my hotel, feeling victorious. Micky will stay the night and let Jimmy sleep. It's the first time he has overnight care in the house, and I hope it will give him comfort.

The next day, Nanee is in bad shape. She didn't sleep well. She demands I read the 23rd Psalm to her and arrange yellow pillows around her head. She says she thinks she's going to die today. I try to reassure her I can take care of everything, from that night's groceries to her funeral plans, but that is not what she needs. She needs to be told that she can die, and I can't bring myself to do that. I'm not ready to. I want my old Nanee back. The one who cracks jokes and watches old reruns of *I Love Lucy*. The one who's feisty and tells me she doesn't need any help. I pull out *The New York Times* Sunday crossword, look at a clue, and say, "Legendary crier."

Nanee wipes her own eyes and says, "Niobe."

"What's Niobe?" I ask.

She says, "The mythological character. The legendary crier. N-I-O-B-E. Here, give me that puzzle!" And my old Nanee returns, just like that.

Later that day, feeling confident that I can care for Nanee myself, I tell Jim to go out and get a beer or take a walk. He finally leaves. Nanee's napping, and I'm catching up on my texts to Brian and Melissa, who need to come say goodbye. While I have my phone in my hand, I glance at Nanee's med schedule. She's long overdue for Ativan, her antidepressant/

antianxiety medicine. I text Jim, asking what the dosage is and if I can give it to her myself.

There's no response from Jim, so I search for Nanee's prescription list and the sheet that says how to administer the drugs. Over the baby monitor, I hear a sound like swishing, so I go into the bedroom to find Nanee hanging, head down, off the bed. A wet brief is on the floor, and she's knocked the tubes out of her nose.

"What happened?" I cry, flying across the room to help her back into bed.

"Leave me alone!" she yells. "I can do this myself!"

She tries to shove me away and nearly falls onto the floor. I wrestle her upright as she demands, "Where's Jim?"

As if on cue, he comes through the door, yelling, "I forgot to give Nanee her Ativan!"

He drops the groceries and jumps in to help. Assured all is under control, I turn away, shaking. The truth is that everything is completely out of my control. I can't do anything in this moment that will help Nanee. I can't cure her ALS. I might not even be able to prevent my own. I mutter that I'm going out for some air. I walk down to the beach. I start calling people who can throw me a lifeline. Kirk and Brian are my go-tos, but nobody's answering. Finally, I call Dadder.

"You didn't do anything wrong," he tells me. "It's not anyone's fault. Jim's doing the best he can, and so are you." There's only love and sympathy in what he's telling me. ALS is a terrible disease, and Nanee is dying the only way she knows how: to fight it to the end. She needs so much help, she wants only Jimmy, and it's too much for him to manage. No wonder he sometimes forgets to give Nanee her medicine.

I feel so helpless, so unhelpful, so frustrated. Nanee would rather crawl out of her bed and break her neck than have me change her diaper.

On the last night of my visit, I sit on Nanee's bed and go through all her jewelry with her again. She's made a comprehensive list of exactly which pieces go exactly where. The Jade Lady to Auntie Melissa. The gold pocket watch to Cousin Elizabeth. The sapphire huggie earrings to Olivia. She makes me pull out her coral suit and a camisole to wear under it. It's her burial outfit. As I go through these rituals, I realize this is the way she can still be in control of the physical world. It's a painful exercise for me; it acknowledges for me this is my last time to see her alive. I don't want to remember her falling out of bed and screaming at me. I want to remember her as the strongest woman I know, my mom.

"This is so hard for me," I admit to her. She looks up from the piles of jewelry on her blanket.

"You have to take all this stuff with you," she says. I shake my head. "No way. You keep it. As long as you're alive, it's still yours."

"Who am I going to impress?" she argues. I think of Brian and Aunt Melissa.

"You'll have more people stopping by. Trust me."

I cannot keep my promise not to cry in front of her. She pats her chest and whispers, "Come here."

I put my head on her chest and cry into her shirt. She

strokes my head for what seems like a long time. I cry all the tears I've held in for four years. Once I've cried myself out, I stand up and dry my face with a tissue. I can't bring myself to say goodbye. As I back out of the bedroom, she says, "You know, I feel in my heart that he's going to be okay."

"Who? Jimmy?" I ask. She shakes her head and says, "Ethan."

I close the door behind me. I fall into Jim's arms right outside the bedroom. He thanks me for coming and tells me he loves me. As he walks me out into the hallway, Micky is on her way in. She hugs me and says that she'll take good care of Nanee. I want to feel relief, but there's no relief for me as long as my mom is suffering.

On my way to the airport, I finally hear back from Aunt Melissa. She says it's not convenient for her to come to Florida right now.

"Do you really think I should come out there?" she asks.

"If you want to see her alive again, you need to come," I explain.

Melissa's on the next flight out. By the time I make my connection in Atlanta, Brian has also committed to come out for a few days after Melissa leaves.

There's nothing left to do on the way back home from the airport, so I call Jim to see how Micky is working out. He tells me Micky is a saint, she respectfully cares for Nanee, and she is more than helpful. He then tells me that when Nanee found out how expensive JT Private Duty nurses were, she fired her.

CHAPTER 17

———◆———

My Hometown

AT 10:17 P.M. on January 9, 2020, I receive this text: *Your Mom passed at 1:01AM. She is now in the Kingdom of heaven. God Bless! Jimmy.*

I tell Kirk, and we cry together on our bedroom floor. Once I collect myself, I text back: *God bless her soul. I am awake if you want to talk.*

I'm okay. Very majestic night as there is a full moon over Sharon and the Gulf. God truly took an angel tonight. I'm glad He blessed me with her for so many years, he texted.

And I reply, *She was blessed to have you. Kirk and I were just talking about how you had so much fun together. She loved you so much.*

The news travels fast. Once I tell Brian and Auntie Melissa, I book myself a flight to Chicago, where Nanee is to be buried. Brian and I will have to work together on all the arrangements, and it's hard to do that from California. Kirk is a star. He makes plans for Ethan to come to Chicago, buys both kids suits and ties, takes off work, and helps me write and rewrite the eulogy.

It's ridiculously cold when I arrive at night in Chicago. Coming back to where I was born is jarring for me. I need to adjust to the weather but also will have to interact with family, some of whom I've not seen for a decade or more. I check into a hotel room with an adjoining suite for Alex and Ethan and try to prepare myself for the coming days. My phone pings and rings. My friends from California are worried about me, but I'm laser focused. Nanee told me exactly what to do, and I'm prepared to do it. When Kirk calls to check in, I tell him that, honestly, I'm at peace with Nanee's passing; I'm relieved that she isn't suffering.

Brian picks me up in the morning, and it's a tonic to be near him. His burly strength and warmth make me feel more comfortable in my cold surroundings. We grab a coffee together before going to the funeral home. Brian is a pillar of our hometown of Highland Park. He seems to know everyone at Starbucks, and they all know our mom died. Total strangers air-kiss me and reassure me they'll be there for the shivah.

We spend the morning at Piser Funeral Home. We go over what color flowers, when Nanee's body will arrive from Florida, where in her family plot she'll be buried, the wording of the obituary, the size and shape of the coffin. Death certificates are promised, and credit cards are charged. There are no tears.

The day is charged with the kind of energy that portends

a large family gathering, and I'm steeling myself to be over-whelmed. Brian drives us back to his house, where I hug my nephews and niece. Brendan, who was particularly close to Nanee, is clearly suffering, and when I ask him how he's hold-ing up, his eyes tear up as he says, "Not well."

The shivah is supposed to be at Brian's the next day, but they're not ready for it. The house still needs a good clean-ing, and the caterer has yet to be contacted. Brian and I are exhausted from the Piser trip, and his wife, Elaine, is busy taking their rambunctious dogs to be boarded. I call Dadder.

"I'll be right over," he promises. Within thirty minutes, he's there to rescue us. He calls his sister, my aunt Barb, who says she'll be over as well. For the next several hours, Brian, Dadder, and I ready the house.

Barb enters, carrying brownies for us. She's arranged so many shivahs that she's an expert. She's already ordered a giant deli plate and bagels from the caterers. My dad looks at me with concern. I'm shaking all over.

Dadder insists on taking me out for a hot tea. For the first time since my mom's death, I feel the numbness and hyperfo-cus crack. I start to cry hard. He just holds my hand and lets me do it. I'm feverish when I stand up.

We all go out to dinner at a Jewish deli that night. I have no appetite and keep sneezing into my matzoh ball soup. Right after dinner, Kirk, Ethan, and Alex arrive. I'm so relieved to see them all, but Kirk hasn't stopped for dinner, and he and the kids are hungry. Once again, I feel like I have to take care of everyone else. The first thing Ethan says to me is, "Wow,

Mom. You're really intense and dramatic tonight. Just chill out, will you?"

I start crying again and don't really stop for two days.

The memorial service is beautiful. There are so many people there who I don't know. People from Jim and Nanee's business. People from her childhood. Students of Nanee's. Cousins, aunts, uncles, Brian's neighbors. They all seem to appreciate my cousin David's presiding over the memorial. Brian, Melissa, and I all get up to speak, and five minutes after the service, I can't remember what we all said, which is probably for the best.

A small group of us, Nanee's immediate family and best friends, go to the gravesite. It's sleeting, and I shiver with fever and misery as they lower her casket into the ground. Aunt Melissa complains loudly that the tractor spilled mud on my grandmother Bubie's headstone. Joey, Nan's friend, cries so hysterically everyone turns around to stare at her. I feel like I'm going to faint.

At the shivah, Jimmy arrives with Joey in tow. He's falling down drunk and wears optic-white sneakers with his gray suit. Joey is still hysterical. I try my best to hold it together, and it helps that Ethan gets up to say a few words about Nanee: "She always told me I can be whatever I want to be and not to give up."

Alex says, "She taught me to always follow my dreams." Everyone pulls me aside to tell me what wonderful boys I have. It's the high point of the weekend. Kirk and the boys go home, and I stay for the final day of shivah. The food is fantastic, and Barb had the foresight to enlist the help of a woman named Judy, who assists with the serving and cleanup. We've cried and visited enough.

The next day, I call Elaine. I ask her to help me recover. She generously brings cold medicine, Advil, and chicken soup to my hotel. I spend the morning recuperating, and by the afternoon, I feel better. My fever finally breaks.

My dad's brother, Uncle Dan, has flown out to Chicago from Montana, and he and Dadder pick me up for an outing. We go to Rosewood Beach, where I used to go with friends in high school. Dan and I stroll the boardwalk and recap the week's events. We agree Nanee would've been thrilled to see all the people who came out and celebrated her. She would've loved the music at the ceremony, savored Aunt Barb's brownies, and laughed at Jimmy for wearing his sneaks with his suit. Since before she and Dadder were engaged, Nanee always had a secret crush on my dad's younger brother. I think it's okay to finally tell him. He says, "I always loved your mom too."

Nanee was the strongest woman I have ever known. Articulate, funny, sensitive, sexy. She was thoughtful, generous, witty, and had integrity. I think a lot of people saw her that way. Even walking on the cold beach with Uncle Dan, I can feel her hand on the back of my head, stroking my hair while she holds me to her chest.

CHAPTER 18

Prepandemic

2020. When I return home, life is mine to live. Kirk and I have planned a getaway to the coast, part of our promise to spend at least a couple of weekends away each year, just us. We have two days to laze around, eat what and when we want, have sex. We do all the above and more. We cry a lot. We talk about Nanee, about the year away from Ethan, about the year since his cancer. We are free from worrying. Suddenly, things seem so much simpler. We sit on the bed in our Pacific-facing room and look out over the ocean. As dismal as it is to be without my mother, life already feels better.

When we get back, I redouble my efforts to get my Congo book published. Although I've been rejected for years, I've never queried publishers directly. After watching Nanee's determination, I'm not about to quit. After four years of limited success with agents, publishers suddenly love me. I have multiple requests for the whole manuscript, and much to my surprise, one request is from an agent. Suddenly, my book is pretty hot shit. I find myself sending the book out to two or more people each day.

Ethan visits home for the first time in late January. The change is obvious. He doesn't fight me over trivial things. If he comes through the door and he doesn't want a hug yet, he says, "Just give me a minute to settle in," rather than, "Back the fuck off, Mom!"

He's more helpful around the house—doing the dishes, walking the dog, and thinking about what would be good for the family and not what's simply good for him. He and Alex, who could barely get along earlier, go out to explore the creeks in town. They play card games and do jigsaw puzzles together.

Because it's the middle of the school year, Alex is busy. He needs to register for high school and present the National History Day play he and his friends have written. Alex has plans to volunteer in the Amigos de las Américas program in Costa Rica; the Spanish immersion excites him almost as much as the environmental activism part. The introductory meeting is slated for the second day of Ethan's visit. Kirk and I both want to go to the meeting with Alex, but we can't leave Ethan home alone yet.

In a tragic turn of events that night, Ethan's elementary school friend Shayne dies from a fall off his balcony after taking hallucinogenic mushrooms. The death shakes us, especially since Shayne's mom, Lisa, had asked me the year before about Gateway and whether I thought it was appropriate for Shayne, who was making "some poor decisions."

"That could've been me," Ethan rightly observes when I tell him about Shayne.

Even though he can get along with us, Ethan's life at home is just a little too unstructured. When he has time on his hands, he gets bored. He's used to the daily practices and structures of school. By the time Eth goes back to school, he's ready to go.

CHAPTER 19

Lipstick

SPRING 2020. Midwinter break comes at a time in the year when parents and kids need it the least. Everyone has their feet back under them after Christmas break and is in the swing of school, and parents rest on the laurels of kids being busy and occupied. Alas, the presidents have to be celebrated, and we need a whole week off to celebrate them. The entire Bay Area seems to head to Tahoe to ski, but some of us don't take to the slopes.

Kirk decides to go fishing over Ski Week, so Alex and I make plans with my friends Margo, Charlie, and their son, Bennett, to go to Tahoe. I hate skiing and so does Alex, so we spend our days snowshoeing and sledding while the James family skies. Halfway through the week, I get a call from someone named Marty who leaves a long, rambling message about how much he loves my book. I have to ask Kirk to check my four-year-old query tracker to find out who Marty is. He owns a publishing company called the Permanent Press, a small independent operation I queried in January.

As Bennett and Alex play guitar duets upstairs, I retreat to my bedroom downstairs and call Marty back. We talk for almost an hour. He says, "I don't know what the fuck everyone else is reading, but I'm reading this!"

I cannot believe, after the hell I've gone through over the past four years, I'm finally getting a break. By the time we hang up, it's clear that not only does Marty like *Unnatural Resources*, but he's going to pay me for it, print it, distribute it, and effectively jump-start my career as a writer. On the drive home, I call all my family members, including Jimmy.

"Nanee works in mysterious ways," he explains. It's a nice sentiment—that my mother has been pulling all the strings that lead to my success or failure, but I know the truth. It's my own hard work, steadfastness, and passion that gets me here. I did this.

I decide, after rewriting the book eleven times over nine years, I'm not going to do any more work on it until I have a contract in front of me.

Nanee lived in three places (Chicago, Florida, and Virginia), and her stuff is everywhere. Jimmy's too wrapped up in the grief of losing her to be bothered with cleaning out her clothes, jewelry, file cabinets, and medical equipment. As soon as he lets me, I fly out to Virginia to help him.

The house has not changed at all since my last visit the previous April. Jim hasn't moved anything of Nanee's. Even her medicine bottles still gather dust on the bathroom counters.

The contents of the refrigerator are laughable. A fifth of vodka, some tonic, half-and-half, a prefab berry and yogurt parfait, and an unopened Boursin cheese spread. My heart breaks for this man who took such loving care of Nanee and now struggles to exist without her. All the furniture that had to be moved against the walls to accommodate her wheelchair still presses the exteriors of each room. There's lots of work to do.

Jim looks awful. He's skinnier and less steady on his feet than ever. I'm nervous about spending ten days with him, especially since the one thing we have in common is now gone. On the day I arrive, he's having his morning coffee in front of Fox News. The headline is about a "Chinese virus" killing people in Wuhan. That it's a big deal doesn't even register to me until he politely switches to MSNBC, which runs the same story.

The sports aftermarket business is Jim's lifeline to sanity, and without Nanee as a business partner, he's free to run the company however he wants. He says it helps keep his loss off his mind. He's home as little as possible when I'm there.

I have decided that I'll be merciless about getting rid of stuff. I only have a week in Virginia, and Nanee'd lived there for thirty years. Unless it has sentimental value to me or my family, it will be consigned to the trash or Goodwill. Once Jimmy leaves for work, I claim the garage for my piles. One for trash, one for Goodwill, one for keeps.

I'm laser-focused again. I hit the bathroom first, keeping good jewelry for family. Everything else goes in the garbage. Nanee wasn't a hoarder, but she seldom threw anything away.

I find aspirin from the 1980s in her medicine cabinet. I find her gold charm from her twenty-first birthday, which proclaims, "You can serve me! I'm legal!"

Next is the walk-in closet. Everything that doesn't fit me goes in the bags for Goodwill. I get so comfortable in her bedroom, I strip down to my underwear with the door open to try her sweaters on. I wrap myself in her bathrobe and inhale. It still smells like her. Turning around in her purple polka-dotted robe, looking in the mirror, I feel like a little girl trying on my mother's clothes. Even though it's a few inches too long in the sleeve, I put it in the "keep for myself" pile.

There's something about giving away her gowns and furs to Goodwill that doesn't sit well with me. Nanee had a strong attachment to her furs; Jack Slade, her uncle, made the coats for her, and her name was monogrammed on the lining. Nanee had a supermodel's body back when she could walk, and even I, an animal lover who hates the idea of wearing a fur garment, can admit there was nothing more elegant than the image of her in a fancy dress, heels, and a fur coat.

I reach out to Carol and Peggy, Jimmy's sisters, for help. They both live in Virginia and know where to put Nanee's finery. Together, we move two cars full of dresses and furs to a consignment shop that donates formalwear to women and girls in military families.

It takes me two more days to get through Nanee's closets and drawers. I find a pair of pantyhose from 1962, still in its cardboard box. I find teddies from her earlier, more naughty years. And when I come across a cute pair of striped socks, I keep them for myself. The most surprising thing I find is in her nightstand. There are at least a dozen half-used bottles of Astroglide lube. I like to think she either still masturbated or she and Jim still had a sex life, even when she was sick.

By far the most wonderful things I find are in her front hall closets. Nanee never let me leave the house without a jacket and a snot rag. In every coat, I find Kleenexes. Everything that's hers has a tissue in the right-hand front pocket. I find myself laughing and crying at the same time, and sometimes, I even use her hankies.

Most of her valuables are in the bonus room above the garage. They're all labeled: Sharon's wedding silver, Sharon's fine china, Sharon's tea set from Annette. It's easy to carry the boxes downstairs, especially since she's already told me where they're going.

Nanee has three deep drawers in the kitchen where she threw every important and unimportant document. In the bottom of one of the drawers, I find her genetic tests for ALS. The doctors have mapped out her entire genome sequence. It's on this document where I'm able to confirm the number of repeats in her C9 expansion. Had I just thrown out everything in the drawer, I would've missed it.

And finally, there are the pictures. There isn't just memorabilia from her lifetime; it goes back generations, from the old country. There are pictures of her father, Milton, who immigrated as a child from Poland. There's Uncle Harry's Purple Heart. There are pictures of Bubie, holding the hand of Aunt Sandy and pregnant with my mom.

There are hundreds of loose pictures from my childhood, and I go through each one, carefully dividing them among Aunt Melissa; cousins Melinda, David, and Elizabeth; Brian; and me.

Each night, Jimmy comes home from work, ready for a V and T. We sit with our cocktails in front of the fire in the den and talk about everything besides politics. I report on the progress I made with my book. He reports on how poorly the business is faring.

We go to dinner every night. I think because Nanee was the cook in the family, he's gotten used to not having to fend for himself. When she got sick, he ordered in. But by the time I get back to Virginia, he's ready to join the ranks of society again. We eat like pigs. Paella at the Spanish restaurant. Sea bass at the country club. Beers and pulled pork at the barbeque place.

After a week there, I find the title to Nanee's car, donate the Steinway baby grand piano to Highland Park High School, and give away all her clothes (besides the robe and the socks, which I keep). Fifty-six garbage bags of clothing go to Goodwill. Nine boxes are shipped to Brian. Six to Melissa. Thirteen to me.

On the last day of packing, Jimmy snaps at me, "How's anyone going to be able to ship this doggone box? It's too heavy, and the tape isn't secure!" I'm so upset with him that I have to excuse myself to go cry in my bedroom. It's been an emotional week, and I think I've done a pretty nice thing to help him out. I don't want to be criticized.

Over dinner at an Italian restaurant, he finally refers to the fact that I've worked seven twelve-hour days to get Nanee's stuff out of his house. He tells me, "Peep, I never would've done that myself. It's just too damned hard."

I'm grateful he acknowledges me.

We fly from Virginia to Florida next. It's so much easier than emptying out their primary residence. The Virginia house is four thousand square feet, and the Florida condo is only an eight-hundred-square-foot apartment. It's also right on the Gulf of Mexico, with 360-degree views of the water. Once we arrive, Jimmy is on vacation. His whole demeanor changes.

"I'd like to live here if I could," he says. I look at the sorry condition into which the condo has fallen. There are vases of decomposing flowers everywhere. Pill bottles, diapers, and rubber gloves clutter the bathroom. Wheelchairs, electric and manual, sit unused in the corners. A walker and a cane lean on the wall in the living room, and a hospital bed takes up half the master bedroom. It looks and smells like someone died there. I only have three days to make the condo livable again. I feel I owe it to Jim.

I call AVOW, the hospice organization in Naples, and arrange for them to pick up the medical equipment. I donate all the clothes, as I had in Williamsburg. All the pills, gloves, and briefs go into the trash. Finally, I realize I'm coming to the end. I spot the ice cream scoop from the house in Highland Park where I grew up and put it into my suitcase. In my last sweep of the condo, a tube of lipstick rolls out from the back of a bathroom drawer. I grab her lipstick, a brick red that used to look great on her, and try it on. It looks pretty good on me too, so I throw it into my purse. It's the closest thing to kissing her goodbye.

CHAPTER 20

Homecoming

MARCH 2020. By the time the boxes arrive at my home in California, COVID-19 has come to the United States. Between unpacking Nanee's pictures, I negotiate my contract with the Permanent Press. Alex's National History Day project is so good his teacher suggests he enter it into the Marin/Sonoma County competition. He and three other boys perform "Don't Lose Your Head: Maximilien Robespierre and the French Revolution," a play he wrote. It's the last group event our family attends before the pandemic shuts everything down. In the fog created by my grief, it hardly registers that the coronavirus is even a big deal. I've been working from home for my entire adult life, so the first few weeks are easy for me. But that changes.

Kirk's office closes, and he starts working from home. It's a transition, having to share an office again, but it's what we have to do. Alex's school abruptly moves to online learning.

Ethan is safe, sheltering in place on the Gateway campus. But with all the support he's gotten at school, he's passing all of the therapeutic levels and classes, and he is getting ready to leave the program. Suddenly, I realize how cluttered our house will be with four people living in it full time. The question of where Ethan will go after he reaches all of the important milestones at Gateway is heavy on our minds. Kirk thinks my reticence about Eth coming home will foil his ability to integrate into the family. It becomes a recurring theme in our conversations. Ethan is afraid I don't want him to come home. Alex is afraid I don't want Ethan to come home. I'm equal parts excited and nervous. While I really miss Ethan, our house has become a peaceful place in his absence. With Nanee resting in peace and Kirk so healthy, I don't want to have to deal with the possibility of disciplining Ethan, arguing with him, or his lying.

At Kirk's urging, I start listening to podcasts about forgiveness. I take Dusty on long walks and listen to podcasts that make me feel like I've been unfair to the men I love. I'm not a man-hater, but the more I hear, the more I realize I harbor grudges against many of the men in my life. I feel like this mistrust is like an anchor around my neck. I resent Dadder for leaving us. I blame Kirk for having cancer and for keeping me in a caretaking role. I mistrust Brian because he won't get the genetic test for ALS. I'm still pissed at the disrespect Ethan showed me for so long. I feel it's getting in the way of my primary relationships. I have to forgive all these men, and I have to forgive myself for carrying these grudges.

That isn't all the preparation we do for Ethan's return. Because he'll be returning to shelter in place with us, he'll need something do keep himself busy. Kirk and I research essential businesses for summer jobs. He'll need something to help him with self-esteem, that has flexible hours and is safe. We research everything from hardware stores to day camps. Ethan needs a new psychologist to help him transition. Matt, his therapist at Gateway, suggests that it be a woman about my age, with kids of her own. This will help Ethan to develop skills to be respectful to me and other females. He'll need a school for the fall, and we've already passed the application deadline for most private schools. Matt suggests because Ethan has been in a thirty-two-person environment, he should find a small school going forward. Something academically rigorous and coed. It's a tall order. The only school like that is the Marin School, and it's pretty selective.

Kirk's high school friend, Nathan, comes through town on a visit. It's fantastic to see him, even if our ability to go to group gatherings is limited. We take advantage of our local sushi restaurant and eat at a socially distanced table. We're the only ones there. The next day, the restaurant permanently shuts down for indoor dining.

My publisher has been unhasty in countersigning my contract. They're a small operation, so things move slowly. I struggle to stop ruminating about my still-unsigned Permanent Press contract, Ethan's pending return, the COVID pandemic, and Alex being waitlisted from San Domenico, his high school of choice. My dad is the eternal optimist about my worries. I turn to him when I am most panicky.

"I find most things that keep me awake usually end up okay," he reasons. Or he'll say, "This too shall pass."

He's right. And I do trust his judgment. I spend several minutes each day meditating on my relationship with him. Yes, he screwed our family up when I was in middle school. Yes, it was painful. But he's also the one I can turn to in a pinch. I rewind through the time we spent on the phone while Nanee was dying. I recall the day he spent with me when we were cleaning up for the shivah. I think about how he flies out every three months to see my kids.

I also meditate on my relationship with Brian. He's my first friend and the only one who really knows what it was like to be raised by such different people. If he decides to stay in the dark about his genetic status, that's his business. I cannot treat him like he's a little kid anymore. It's not my job. I don't take the relationship for granted, and I vow to be supportive rather than judgmental.

And I need to forgive Kirk, the love of my life. I look back on all the years we've had together. In the first fifteen years of marriage, we've weathered cancer twice, buried two parents, seen Ethan through his tumultuous teenage years, and endured two generations of ALS. We've also had so much fun. We've hardly ever missed a weekly date night. We've traveled around the world together, made movies together, and supported each other's dreams. We said so many things over the last few years that we regretted. But we've never stopped loving each other.

On Mother's Day, I receive a poignant letter from Ethan.

Mom,

This year, I wanted to stray from the past and aim for the future. I know our relationship hasn't always been smooth sailing, and it usually forced you into a pretty rough spot. When I come home, you'll be putting trust in new bonds that we've been creating over the past year. After all the second chances, this one is really important, and I'm so grateful that you worked so hard with me. You are so, so smart. Smart about your struggles, smart about your interests, and smart about our family. I can't describe how much that means to me. Your steadfast nature is about to get your book on the shelves, it got Dad through cancer (twice), and it helped me throughout my therapeutic journey. As a cornerstone for lots of people, I don't think anyone could fill your shoes. The greatest gift I could give this Mother's Day would be to come home and be a part of a happy, healthy household. I can't wait to be there and give you a big hug (while stooping a little . . .).

So much love, Ethan

I smile at how much Ethan has grown up. He understands his role in the family and he appreciates that I love him.

Alex gets into San Domenico the next week, just as he goes through a drive-through commencement from White Hill Middle School. The graduation from junior high is less than glorious. He's handed a diploma by masked teachers who reach into our car window with gloved hands.

I start reaching out to more organizations who are invested in longitudinal ALS research. I put my name on waiting lists at Columbia University, Harvard, University of Miami, ALS Therapy Development Institute, and the NIH, with the hope that once there is a COVID vaccine, I can fly out and participate. I read websites for nonprofits that help ALS patients. I subscribe to ALS newsletters. I learn everything I can about the C9orf72 mutation and am shocked that all ALS patients aren't given a genetic test to determine whether their disease is inherited.

My book contract arrives, fully executed. The Permanent Press promises a November release of *Unnatural Resources*. I hire my friend Laurel to oversee PR for the book launch. Shannon, my writing partner, suggests Alison Bricker, who creates a beautiful website.

Then Ethan returns home. Not only do he and I get along, but he is affectionate, respectful, and kind. He and Alex are suddenly best buddies, walking the dog together, going out for ice cream, playing cards, and bike riding together. Ethan applies for a job at ACE Hardware in their soils and nursery department, and he gets the job. The boost to his ego is immediate, and he's excited to go to work each day. Ethan starts to take drivers ed classes online. Within six weeks, he and I go to the DMV for his learner's permit. The Marin School provisionally accepts him, on the condition he continues to do well at home. We'll have to wait to find out if he'll be attending.

"It's okay, Mom. I've learned about delayed gratification," he says. And he has learned. Fifteen months of residential treatment have taught him hard work will pay off, even if the payoff is delayed.

"You've got this, Ethie. Look how well you're doing. Look how well we're doing together," I say.

CHAPTER 21

June Getaway

SUMMER 2020. I am out of town, alone for the first time since the coronavirus hit four months ago. The property where the cottage sits boasts acres of manicured gardens, flowing waterfalls, and towering redwoods. It used to be the drawing studio of Charles Schulz. The breeze stirs the leaves of a Japanese maple where a yellow finch chirps. It's the physical embodiment of the peace I feel at this point of my life. Kirk has been cancer-free for almost two years. I don't feel like I need to watch over my shoulder for his approaching monster of illness anymore. Nanee, God rest her soul, is wherever the best of us go. Alex continues to fill our house with music and laughter. And Ethan, who bends from his six-foot-two-inch frame to hug me, is a respectful, happy young man. I plan to go camping with him in August, and for the first time, I look forward to spending a weekend alone with him.

My novel, *Unnatural Resources*, after ten years, has been published. I'm delighted to see that it's already listed for presale on the Amazon website. I plan to have an in-person book launch in the fall. It's the first live event I've heard of in months. I visualize a covered, open-air affair, with people seated six feet apart. A livestream of the launch will have to be available for those who are uncomfortable with a potentially super-spreading event. It's not going to be indoors, like a normal book launch, but I'll be damned if I'm going to let a pandemic spoil my book birthday. I've worked way too long for coronavirus to rain on my parade.

With so many things finding resolution around me, the words in this memoir come easier to me. To sit under a maple tree and contemplate the enormity of the last few years is a gift to myself. As the paragraphs appear on the page, I silently resolve to find more like-minded people. Where are all of the other presymptomatic C9 gene carriers? Certainly, I can't be the only one who's had a positive genetic result in the absence of symptoms. Don't others feel the same way I do: their lives and their kids' lives are being threatened by this pathogenetic ninja?

I've heard of this organization called I AM ALS, a patient-centric group that provides community for ALS patients and their caregivers. They do everything from advocacy to mentoring. Without being a symptomatic patient or a caregiver, I fall through many cracks in the ALS community, but this organization has a familial ALS cohort, and I plan to join when I get home from the Schulz cabin.

Dadder and I have decided to help fund two research studies. One is the development of a C9 ALS drug at the ALS Therapy Development Institute—the only nonprofit lab dedicated to ALS research. The other is ongoing research into C9 ALS by a young doctor at UCSF named Paul Sampognaro. This kind of involvement helps Dadder stay connected to the fight against hereditary ALS. During a pandemic, it's really the only way he can.

The scary, fanged, toothy monster of ALS still lives under my bed. I'm not ready to tell my kids about it; with Nanee's death and their dad's cancers, it's still too much. I meet on Zoom with neurologists, participate in genetic studies, and add my story to longitudinal research. The time will come someday when I will be called on to do battle with this monster. I look forward to it. Without the worries of the past five years, I have much more bandwidth. I've learned there are times to surrender: when your mom declines care or when your brother ignores his genetic risks. And there are times to fight like hell: when you start feeling weakness in your extremities or when your speech starts to slur. I'm not there yet, but I'm ready. I'll do everything in my power to make sure that my kids and their children do not die of ALS. Unlike Nanee, I know the monster before it notices me. I will fight it with everything I have. I will win.

CHAPTER 22

Synapses

IT'S NOVEMBER 17, 2021. Today marks the one-year anniversary of the release of *Unnatural Resources* on Amazon, and I couldn't be more proud. I just hung a framed winner's certificate next to my desk in my office. My novel has won praise from Adam Hochschild, *Publisher's Weekly*, and *The Library Journal*. Since its launch last year, it also won Honorable Mention at the San Francisco Writer's Fest, but this win is really exciting: it's the NYC Big Books Award for Cultural Heritage. To be an award-winning novelist means so much to me because I put ridiculous amounts of passion, time, money, and work into this first book. And I did it while juggling some of the hardest challenges of my life. I feel strong, capable, and deserving of praise. In fact, the energy boost I get from the success of my novel has encouraged me to work on other forms of writing. Several of my essays are up on the I AM ALS website. I've entered

ALS essays into contests, spoken about ALS to classes of nurses, and appeared on panels. I've also taught classes on querying and determination. I've taught several high school classes about being a humanitarian writer. And in the last two weeks, I've been accepted into writing workshops in Wisconsin and Guatemala and residencies in Georgia and New York. Writer's conferences and residencies love my underdog's story.

My stepdad, Jimmy, died a year ago, just nine months after Nanee passed away. The cancer he'd neglected during the years of caretaking an ALS patient finally caught up with him. I can romanticize it all I want, thinking that he died of a broken heart or that they're in heaven together. But I know better. He died because he didn't take care of himself. He died because he put her care first.

Right after Jimmy passed away, Biden and Harris took over the helm of our country. With a COVID vaccine on the way to the general public, the possibility of travel became a reality.

I connected with my aunt Melissa after Nanee and Jimmy died. She taught me Tai Chi via Zoom, and we spent hours talking about my mom and ALS and the possibility that Melissa had the gene mutation for C9orf72. Melissa has two kids and four grandchildren. I urged her to get on the same waiting lists I was on, but she, like Brian, preferred to live in ignorance over knowing about any potential scratching monsters under her mattress.

In December of 2020, UCSF finally contacted me to participate in their live ALLFTD-ARTFLS study, a longitudinal research project of genetic ALS carriers and their families. I began taking tests and doing interviews via Zoom. Then I was called in to do several MRIs. Researchers can learn a lot about ALS progression by studying brain transformations over time. Then I heard from DIALS, Harvard's dominant ALS study at Massachusetts General Hospital. We agreed that I would participate in their longitudinal research once it was safe for me to fly. I crossed my fingers and prayed to get my COVID vaccine. The last thing I wanted was to catch coronavirus on an airplane and bring it home to my husband who had only two years prior gone through six months of chemotherapy.

At I AM ALS, I am part of their Familial ALS Team, a member of their Clinical Trials Team, and a peer support mentor. I've made friends—other gene carriers of ALS. They're all parents, and many of them were able to conceive children without the ALS gene, through IVF. We talk every week about how to get gene carriers enrolled in clinical trials. We share information about ongoing research and advocacy.

I also joined Everything ALS, which does longitudinal research through their Speech Study Program. Every week I record my voice to watch for changes in speech patterns (and also to bank my voice for safekeeping in case I need it later).

My first public reading of *Unnatural Resources* was in February of 2021, online at the Larkspur Public Library. A month later, I got my first COVID vaccine. As my book was taking off, so was my life as a research participant. It was time for me to tell my kids about the C9orf72 gene.

We were sitting at the table, eating dinner, and I said, "I'm going to Boston soon."

Alex asked why. I said it was to participate in medical research around ALS, the disease that Nanee had. They already knew that I had been part of a longitudinal study at UCSF for "people with ALS in their families," but they didn't yet know I had the gene. I said sometimes, in a small percentage of cases, ALS ran in families, so when Nanee was diagnosed, I went to have the genetic test. Ethan asked, "Do you have the gene?"

"Yes, I do, but it doesn't mean that I will get ALS, and the reason I'm doing research is so we can find a cure before I develop any symptoms."

I wasn't lying, but I did omit that the vast majority of C9 gene carriers either develop ALS or FTD. I also omitted the average age of onset is about fifty-five. They didn't need to know that; they just needed to know I was doing something about it.

"I'm going to donate blood, urine, spit, and spinal fluid over the next several years. I'll also need to fly to Boston every six months. The study at MGH also includes strength tests, speech tests, and cognitive tests. I'll be doing the same stuff at UCSF over the next few years."

"Can I get tested for the ALS gene?" Ethan asked. I told him honestly that kids don't get ALS, but if he wanted to get tested, he could once he turned eighteen. That satisfied him. Alex was noticeably quiet. He was taking in that I carried a deadly disease, but I wasn't sure he understood he had a chance of being a genetic carrier until he thanked me for making sure they didn't get it.

I received my second COVID vaccine in April and flew to Boston to participate in DIALS in May. Dadder flew out to meet me. It was the first time we'd seen each other since Nanee's funeral fifteen months prior. Seeing Dadder was like a gift. Not only was I instantly reassured he would weather the pandemic, but I had someone who loved me who could hold my hand through difficult appointments. Sadly, Harvard's policy was to not allow any visitors with research participants. It was just too risky because COVID was everywhere. Dadder and I would have to content ourselves with just seeing each other at the hotel and for meals.

At Mass General Hospital, I met Dr. Katie Nicholson, a neurologist at DIALS. She was so excited to meet me she rolled back and forth on her chair as she went over the consent forms with me. We talked about gene testing, and her research assistant came in to do some cognitive tests on me. I recited the alphabet and listed all the words I could that started with the letter f. I listed all the animals I could think of in a minute. Another doc assessed my gait, my reflexes, and the strength in my muscles, including my tongue. I gave a urine sample. I had my blood pressure checked, my temperature taken.

I found myself wondering if they were ever going to tell me anything about my health. The MRI scanner was on the fritz, which meant that Dr. Nicholson couldn't look at the imaging of my brain. I was told that if they couldn't get the scanner working, I'd have to return within forty-five days. Otherwise, the first round of cognitive tests would be invalid.

I loved Katie. She and her assistants treated me with respect. When I asked her why she did such challenging work on an incurable, fatal disease, she said it was because of people like me. I noticed she wasn't wearing a wedding ring. Did that mean she wasn't married? Did it mean she was without kids? It didn't surprise me. She treated her work like it was her life. I really didn't mind returning a month later. And I still don't mind flying out there. I am committing to participate in this research until they find a cure.

Kirk continues to be healthy. It's been three years since his last chemo treatment, and he lives in life-affirming ways. He goes mountain biking. He does yoga. He loves his fly-fishing trips. And he's finally building a fishing cabin of his own. It's in Sierra City, just steps away from good fishing spots and an hour from the ski slopes.

He and I are going on a getaway next month to Sonoma, near where we were married. We'll discuss our twenty-year anniversary, which is coming up. Assuming COVID allows us to, we'll be traveling to Paris next year, just the two of us.

Kirk, Ethan, Alex, and I spent our first vacation together in two years in Kauai. It was such a difference, traveling with a family that could peacefully coexist.

Ethan has continued to amaze us. Not only has he kept his job at ACE, but he's also maintained good grades at the Marin School. He got his driver's license just a few months ago and bought himself a car. After working with a college counselor and visiting several campuses, he applied Early Action to three schools. The University of Oregon will welcome him next fall, and he'll study product design. It wasn't easy for him to achieve all these goals. In fact, some of the lessons he's learned have come painfully. He and Alex were arrested last October for trespassing and had to go through the Youth Restorative Justice program. It took them weeks of juvenile online teenage jury duty and cleaning up McNears Beach to clear their records. And Ethan has discovered pot and alcohol again since getting his driver's license and a car. Kirk and I continue to white-knuckle our way through parenting him, but he's an adult, and he needs to learn how to be a responsible one. We're done intervening in his life. He will have to deal with his successes and failures as an adult.

Alex continues to be a tenderhearted and talented child. He spent part of last summer volunteering with the Amigos de las Américas program in Nicaragua. His proficiency in languages and his humanitarian heart, coupled with his innate interest in exploring unfamiliar places, made him popular on that trip. He excels in a high school where he was new last year. San Domenico is a rigorous education compared to public school, and he's taking honors classes, playing guitar in the school rock band, and riding with the mountain bike club. His sweetness and good looks have the attention of the kids around him, and he has a ton of friends in the neighborhood. I cherish the time I have with him, and I am looking forward to upcoming adventures with my second son. We've taken several trips together—mostly to houses on the coast that we rented—and we spend our time listening to music together, eating good food, and walking on the beach.

The monster under my bed has become a friend. Sometimes I hear it snarling or scratching, but it is part of my life. I know that it can't really hurt me. If I develop symptoms of ALS tomorrow, I will find a way to train this monster. The doctors who I see and the research I'm participating in will give me tools. It's been an exercise in letting go of fear of my own body. Five years ago, I didn't understand that loving myself means also loving the ALS gene that I carry. Five years ago, it was hard to imagine that my life would become a joy. Now I recognize my own resilience, my own stores of strength, and I realize that my life—monster or no monster—is a gift.

CHAPTER 23

A Note on Victory

AUGUST 26, 2022. It's my fifty-third birthday. I'm enjoying a crab roll at Fish restaurant in Sausalito. The sun is shining through the glass of sauvignon blanc on my picnic table. My hand is steady, still free from fasciculations as I reach for the lemon wedge to squirt on my crab sandwich. There's a breeze coming off the water that sets moored sailboats rocking. The wind blows my gray-streaked hair into my face. I smile at the internal acknowledgment that the gray strands mark the years I've survived genetic ALS, while the brown ones mark the years I will potentially live.

Last week, I sat on a patient advisory committee to the National Institutes of Health (NIH). The topics proposed were federal grants given to three ALS drug studies. Since President Biden signed the ACT for ALS bill into law this year, the government has committed to allotting millions of dollars for research into drugs to combat ALS and other rare, fatal neurodegenerative diseases. It was the NIH's job to advise the Food and Drug Administration about granting expanded access for ALS patients to enroll in clinical trials for drugs that were still in development. As a patient advocate, it was my job to tell the NIH about the potential benefits to presymptomatic patients. It was an honor to serve in this capacity—to help patients access lifesaving medicine that can keep ALS at bay.

Last month, after years of my pestering her, Aunt Melissa finally got tested for the C9 gene. She's a carrier. At seventy-two, she's lucky to not have any symptoms yet. She may be one of the percentage of people with the mutation that will live without ALS or FTD. Melissa's unhappy about her diagnosis, but she knows that her grandkids can someday make informed decisions about having kids of their own. Hopefully, her kids will get tested too. As disappointed as I am about her test results, I'm reassured to have a fellow warrior in the battle against this monster disease.

I recently read an article about a prophylactic mRNA vaccine for C9orf72 that's being developed in Europe. Human trials for this vaccine are on the horizon within the next five years. This is a game changer for carriers of ALS gene mutations. For me, it gives me hope that C9 ALS will someday be like my high cholesterol; I might have it, but I can control it with lifestyle changes and medicine, and it won't kill me.

I still wear a silver monogrammed necklace that says PEEP. It was the last gift that Nanee gave me before she died. I raise my glass to my mother, take a sip of wine, and dig in.

Epilogue

―――――◆―――――

IT'S APRIL 16, 2023. I've just signed the consent form to participate in a clinical trial of riluzole in premanifest ALS patients. In the five years since I received my genetic results, I've gone from study to study, begging any researcher who will listen to please consider me and my familial ALS cohort as patients, as worthy of a shot at survival. In early 2023, several Familial Team members at I AM ALS decided to form a nonprofit of our own. We call ourselves End the Legacy, and we're all carriers of genes that cause ALS and FTD. My friends, Jean Swidler, Julie Granning, Tucker Olson, and I all testified to the FDA about our rights to participate in drug trials to prophylactically stave off our fatal disease. For the first time, the FDA was forced to confront the reality: there are thousands of premanifest gene-carrying patients who will die of ALS and FTD without medical intervention.

The DIALS study at Massachusetts General Hospital is recruiting two presymptomatic ALS patients for a trial of a repurposed rheumatoid arthritis drug, baricitinib, to see if it can prevent neuroinflammation and disease progression. I was screened for the trial but didn't qualify because I have diverticulitis, and it's an exclusion criterion. Thankfully, another member of End the Legacy will be able to participate. ETL has a great ally in Dr. Terry Heiman-Patterson, a neurologist at Temple University who believes that all premanifest ALS patients should be on an ALS drug. End the Legacy is part of her nonprofit, ALS Hope. With all of these advances, I still didn't feel like things were moving fast enough. Sometimes I would get a cramp in my toe. Sometimes my left quadriceps would twitch, and I could all but feel the monster's rank breath on my face. I began to think that there was a chance I may not live to see a cure.

I reached out to Synapticure, I AM ALS's for-profit arm, whose mantra is to help ALS patients who fall through the cracks of the medical system. Although patients have to pay for their service, Synapticure at least hears what they have to say. I explained that without trial enrollment, presymptomatic patients have no hope for survival. I met with a neurologist, Dr. Faber, online, and he got it. We agreed to work together to write a proposal for a trial of the oldest ALS drug, riluzole. It's been around since 1995, has few side effects, and extends the lifespan of ALS patients. I double-checked with the doctor who discovered the C9orf72 gene, Bryan Traynor, about the safety and effectiveness of riluzole. Like most other neurologists I've spoken to, he'd never considered it for premanifest gene carriers, but he thought it was safe. I spoke with my own neurologist, Paul Sampognaro, at UCSF. He also thought it was worth a try. While Dr. Faber was working on IRB approval, I received an email from the National Academies of Sciences, Engineering, and Medicine.

The National Academies have been around since Abraham Lincoln was president, and they work on big problems by assembling committees and writing reports for the government. When Biden signed ACT for ALS into law, Congress and the NIH worked to put together a path forward to make ALS a livable disease. They hired the National Academies to assemble an eighteen-person committee to work over two years, writing a report it would later submit to Congress. They interviewed me and ninety-nine other experts in ALS (neurologists, biotech company CEOs, geneticists, ALS patients, ethicists, and researchers). In the end, they chose me to represent the genetic ALS community. I felt humbled, honored, and excited to be chosen. Every other month for the next two years, I'll meet with my fellow committee members in Washington, DC, and together we'll work on a report on how to make ALS a livable disease within the next ten years. I plan to push hard for premanifest patients' rights: genetic counseling and testing; access to ALS drugs; enrollment in clinical trials. And I plan to be the loudest person in the room.

The consent form from Synapticure landed in my inbox yesterday. Tomorrow, I'll go over the form and sign it over Zoom. For the longest time, I told myself that it honors Nanee when I participate in research. I also told myself I was doing battle with the monster for my kids. Both of these things are true, but it's also true I'm doing it for me. I like the feeling of jumping rope, of singing at the top of my lungs, of hugging my husband with strong arms. I enjoy chewing delicious food, walking outside to feel the breeze on my skin, using my hand to fill in the boxes of *The New York Times* crossword puzzle. It's not selfish to want to keep all of my bodily functions. I want things for myself: to see my grandchildren, to travel to Japan and Greece, to see this book published.

This war of nerves I'm engaged in never gives me a break. When I got my genetic test results, when I decided to do something about them, I enlisted in a never-ending battle. Now, I don't ever get a vacation from ALS. Although I've learned to accept this monster, it doesn't mean I want to live with it. Five years ago, when I heard the monster scratching on the underside of my bed, I said I'd flip up the mattress and blow the motherfucker off the planet with an Uzi, and I didn't really know what that meant. Now, as I read the consent form, I realize that I'm holding a much bigger gun. If I can stave off the symptoms of ALS long enough, the gene editing vaccine may become a reality in time for me to benefit from it.

Over the years, I've cried a lot of tears. Tears of frustration when I didn't think Ethan was making progress. Tears of terror at watching Kirk suffer from cancer. Tears of grief at losing Nanee. And now, as I read through the consent, I cry a different kind of tears: tears of hope.

Acknowledgments

There are so many people who helped me along my C9 journey. Sit back and settle in; this is a long list! Several of my most admired champions are from the medical and nonprofit world, and all are part of my growing community. Heaping hugs go to Jean Swidler, Daniel Barvin, Cassandra Haddad, Tucker Olson, and all my friends at Genetic ALS and FTD: End the Legacy for giving me a place to call home. For teaching me how to really listen, I thank the peer mentors and mentees at I AM ALS. For early support and a place to put my voice, I appreciate Indu Navar and EverythingALS.

Thanks go to ALS TDI, especially Fernando Vieira, Clare Reich, and Glynis Murray, for lifesaving research and inspiration. Synapticure made it possible for me to be one of the lucky presymptomatic ALS patients to go on riluzole. It's a crazy idea, but it just might work! I'm proud to be patient number one at the Bluefield NSP, and Hope Horton did a great job of collecting my blood every three months for these last few years. Thanks go to the DIALS study at Mass General for inviting me to participate in such a meaningful way. The ALLFTD study at UCSF has been monitoring my progress, or lack thereof, for years. I thank them for keeping an eye on me and for their patience with my Stroop Color and Word Test results. I'm studying beforehand next time! My sunny disposition and pluck would be severely affected were it not for my bright, optimistic neurologist, Paul Sampognaro. I enjoy brainstorming with him and appreciate his respectful bedside manner.

I thank the staff at the National Academies of Sciences, Engineering, and Medicine for asking me to help author the "Living with ALS" report. They and my fellow committee members made me feel heard, even though I have no letters after my name. Making ALS a livable disease was a tall order, and it was such a pleasure to collaborate with them all. The folks at the National Institute of Neurological Disorders and Stroke's neurodegenerative disorders study, especially Bryan Traynor and Justin Kwan, treated me like I was contributing to something great when they collected my data and shared my results back. I thank them for their hard work on genetic ALS and FTD.

What can I say about the Honeybadgers? I've never seen a group of such ferocious, determined, like-minded people get together to get things done. What a movement! I'm proud to be a part of it. *Rawr!*

I am indebted to the National Institute of Neurological Disorders and Stroke, who invited me to deliver the keynote address at the 2024 Nonprofit Forum. How great to have a genetic mutation carrier front and center. Roon asked me tough questions about ALS and featured me on their app. This is a powerful tool for people to get answers and demystify this fatal disease.

I thank Jacinda Sampson for delivering the news of my monster in a gentle, understandable way. I thank Diane Lucente for explaining genetics and for explaining them in a warm, empathetic way. Pamela McDonald taught me about the APOE gene diet and got me off caffeine, dairy, alcohol, refined sugar, and red meat. I appreciate her and admit to faltering occasionally.

Matt Jackman at Gateway Academy treated Ethan with empathy and dignity in his darkest hours. I thank Matt for being in his court and for helping us bring him home. Jen Lucas, the "Lymphomaniac," gets credit for bringing Kirk back from the brink. Erin, Nanee's caregiver, and Carly, Nanee's social worker from Avow, supported our family up until the end. I thank them for their kindness.

There will never be a Honeybadger like Sandy Morris. She is still my hero. May she rest in peace.

There are so many organizations, writing mentors, and residencies who supported me on my writing adventure. I thank Millay Arts, the Hambidge Center, Corsicana Residency's Writers House, and Madison Writers' Studio (especially editor Susannah Daniel). I am grateful to Joyce Maynard and

Janis Cooke Newman for giving me a comfortable place to write and for providing me with a robust community of fellow authors and artists to call my friends. I'd be a total loser without the Write On Mamas and the Page Street writers.

For enduring friendship, I thank Shannon Takaoka and Dorothy O'Donnell. For excellent feedback and support, I thank Marianne Lonsdale, Rina Neiman, Evelyn Weiser, and Jessica O'Dwyer. I appreciate Daniel Sheih, Ly Tran, Preeti Parikh, and Leslie Lindsay for writing letters of recommendation, being my lovely housemates, and lending a hand when I needed one. I thank Jenny Barry for walking with Dusty and me, for giving sage advice about publishing, for helping me lawyer up, and for shared deliciousness.

Thanks go to Book Passage, the Pacific Northwest Writers Association Conference, Kathy Hagee, the Hivery, the San Anselmo Library, the Larkspur Library, *The Women's Eye*, and *Elephant Journal* for allowing me to talk about activism, querying, and the life of an author.

A shout-out goes to my creative nonfiction group at Page Street. Mary Rosenthal, Young Whan Choi, and Jihii Jolly saw me through the final draft of this book. I thank them for their friendship and eagle eyes!

Thanks go to Justin Branch, Jen Glynn, Rebecca Logan, and all at Greenleaf Book Group for believing in my ability to tell this story. Here's to the start of a beautiful friendship.

I'm so blessed to have close friends and family members who helped me keep my sanity during the whirlwind between 2018 and 2022. In no particular order, they are Cynthia

Stanley, Debby Rice, Arthur Kessler, Laura Bloch, Margo James, Rhian Robinson, Scott Fay, Yago Fidani, MaryBeth McClure, Beth Touchette, Maria Dudley, Becca Douglass, Laurie Boscoe, Marie Henrio, Jenny Terry, Carroll Cannon, and Peggy Crowder. I love them all.

Resources

Here are some things you can do to help find a cure for ALS and FTD:

- Go to the I AM ALS website, https://www.als.org, to learn about legislation to help ALS community members.

- Attend a Lou Gehrig Day event at your favorite ballpark. Information is available at https://www.als.org.

- Watch *Go On, Be Brave*, a movie about the resilience of PALS. Information can be found at https://www .goonbebravefilm.org.

- Educate yourself about FTD at AFTD's website: https://www.theaftd.org.

- Donate to ALS TDI to help fund lifesaving research: https://www.als.net.

- Participate in the Ice Bucket Challenge at https://www.als.org.

- As a healthy volunteer, add your voice to Everything ALS's speech study. Information is at https://www.everythingals.org.

- Check out the End the Legacy website to advocate for people with genetic variants at https://www.endthelegacy.org.

- Donate to the ALS Hope Foundation and direct your gift to End the Legacy. Info at https://www.alshf.org/end-the-legacy.

- Write a review of this book on https://www.amazon.com and https://www.goodreads.com.

About the Author

Photo by Kathleen Harrison

MINDY UHRLAUB is a founding member of End the Legacy. Her debut novel, *Unnatural Resources*, won the 2021 NYC Big Book Award for Cultural Heritage. Mindy also received the 2025 Harvey and Bonny Gaffen Advancements in ALS Award from the Les Turner ALS Foundation. She lives in Northern California with her family.

Follow Mindy at MINDYUHRLAUB.COM, on X @MINDYUHRLAUB, and on Instagram @MINDYWRITES1.